Desert in My Backyard: One Woman's Journey into Silence

By Jeanne Lound Schaller

Introduction

Catherine House sits hidden until I am almost upon it. Its mute presence speaks about the goodness of silence, even when I'm not conscious of it being there. It whispers and echoes throughout the pages of this book, often invisible yet always present, an indispensable part of my spiritual journey.

Thirty-six years ago we built Catherine House, a prayer house, near the far end of our ten country acres. I go there often, attempting to get in touch with and be touched by silence; the silence that is present as a blessed relief when I seek temporary respite from this noisy world, and the deeper Silence that is God.

Quietness is a key element that has stimulated my growth into an adult faith, seeds which were planted in my childhood through observing my mother kneeling in prayer by her bed at night and hearing her talking quietly with God as she worked about the house; simple gestures like my father helping us in the fields and orchards after he had worked all day at his regular job. I was affirmed by his gentle, often quiet presence, and work wasn't nearly so hard when Dad joined us in our labors.

This book shares stories within a story, relating how Catherine House came to be built and how my sojourns there have shaped and continue to shape my life. It includes sketches of me as woman, wife, mother, grandmother, mediator and peace activist and how opening myself to silence and to Silence has enriched and refined my vision about life and my understanding of how I am to live it as a person who claims to be a Christian. This little house is an indispensable part of my journey.

These pages also share my poetry as well as glimpses of several of the hundreds of visitors who have been blessed to spend a few minutes, hours or days at Catherine House.

Also included is my deep distress - in my mid-50s - about the Catholic Church and how questioning and questing through lengthy discernment led me to my new home in the Midland Church of the Brethren. The final stories focus on a four-week retreat and a three-month Bangkok Adventure as an International Rotary Peace Fellow at age 68. Both experiences nourished my hope that in my elder years I will be able to "Dance in the Cosmos Without a Script."

Acknowledgements

Feelings run deep regarding each of these people:

Delight that artist and granddaughter Chloe Ann Schaller created the picture on the cover.

Gratitude to those in whose cottage or homes I spent many days writing while they were away: Eric and Kelly Krause, Betty and Rich Meyette, Skip Renker and Julia Fogarty, Ann and Guy Skabardis, Dave and Linda Z. Smith, Jim and Kathy Sullivan, Judy Timmons and Tom and Amy Tolton.

Appreciation for those who read the manuscript. Getting feedback was invaluable: Pauline Bednarick, Catalina Echeverri, Sandy Fix, Pat Lynott, Janet Martyn, Ann Schaller Skabardis, Judy Timmons and Cris Wyns and anyone else who helped in any way. Judy not only read and reread, she also spent countless hours helping edit and format, using her many techie skills that are far beyond my abilities.

Thankfulness for Paul and Alice Owens who let us take apart an old house on their land so we could build a new one on ours. Their generosity has been a blessing to hundreds of visitors.

jgschall@outlook.com

Chapters

A Little Desert - A Resting Place in God

I have a desert in my backyard. It's surrounded by poplars, pines and maples on the far end of our ten acres, five miles from downtown Midland, Michigan. This sacred space is Catherine House, a poustinia, (pooh-stin'-ee-uh) a Russian word for "little desert" where I have often gone both to seek and to immerse myself in silence. The path that takes me there winds past white pines and birches. Sometimes a deer darts across in front of me. Occasionally when I've gone very early or have spent the night there, I've been blessed to see one quietly feeding in the morning mist.

Catherine de Hueck Doherty, a baroness prior to Russia's revolution, introduced the concept of poustinia to Madonna House, a training center for the lay apostolate that she and her husband, Eddie, founded in Combermere, Ontario, Canada, in 1947. Catherine, affectionately known as "The B", was a woman of great prayer and vision who had been raised in a deeply Christian home with both Orthodox and Roman Catholic influences. She often accompanied her mother when she visited the poustiniki who lived in a hut in the woods. As a result of her upbringing, Catherine created her own poustinia in her heart at a young age and carried it with her as she grew up, then emigrated to North America to escape from Russia. She understood that it would take plenty of time for the Western mind to embrace the concept of sitting entirely alone with God in solitude in a secluded space. Thus, it was decades later that the first poustinia's door was opened at Madonna House.

I made my first trip there in 1967 as a student at Aquinas College, run by the Dominican Sisters in Grand Rapids, Michigan. Fr. Sharkey, the college chaplain, accompanied several students to northern Ontario during winter break. That brief visit affected me profoundly. I was inspired by the life of community, prayer, simplicity and outreach to the poor. I was pleased that the concept of mission in that community meant attempting to live the Gospel, rather than converting others to Christ.

Even at 20, I was drawn to the idea of taking only a loaf of bread, a jug of water and the Bible and spending twenty-four hours in silence with God in a tiny hut with a strange name. When I first asked to do this, on a return visit to Madonna House a couple years later, Fr. Briere embarrassed and disappointed me by saying I should simply spend time in the chapel instead. The reason he gave is forgotten, but it was a painful moment. A much later visit in 1985 did include poustinia time, but by then I already had a desert in my own backyard.

I met my husband, George, on that first trip to Madonna House. He went at the invitation of a friend. At that point he had his eye on a perky redheaded Irish gal, who also made the trip. Long story short, we were married in December 1968 and moved to Midland in 1971 with our daughter, Ann Marie. We talked about building our own poustinia for years, but city living with a small backyard didn't allow it. In 1978 we moved to the country with our four children, the youngest still in a baby pack, into a before-the-turn-of-the-century farmhouse that needed a major labor of love. For three years we poured ourselves into working on the house while holding onto the thought that on our long, narrow acreage that was mostly open land, a young poplar grove near the back end would be the perfect spot for a long-awaited dream to be realized.

When we first moved here we planned to use one room in our home as a prayer space, an idea that was dropped when my sister, Catherine, came to live with us that same year. Instead, a corner of our bedroom sufficed. After George,

Catherine, and our older children, Ann Marie and Peter, left in the mornings, I would sit there for an hour devouring spiritual books. Matthew and Christopher came in and out, climbing into my lap or just whispering little messages to me. This worked well for a year or two but there was a growing hunger within me for something more. Then, as I've learned, as often happens when we move in God's time, things just fell into place.

God's Timing

In the spring of 1981, we decided the coming summer was the time to build. Our good friend, Hugh, estimated it would cost $1400 to construct a 12'x18' building including a screened in porch. We couldn't afford that, so putting practical matters aside, we moved in faith. This was to be a community project, both in its creation and its usage. I wrote letters to twenty friends, sharing our vision and inviting them to donate time, money or materials. We asked for small donations, expecting to raise only a portion of what we needed. I'm sure Hugh was right in his estimated cost, but another possibility presented itself.

One morning that spring I was riding my bike south of our land, past an old, tiny, boarded-up house about a quarter mile down the road. It had been vacant for years and was an eyesore. I had never given it much thought. That morning when I glanced at it, "poustinia" popped into my mind. It kept running around my brain, so I contacted the neighbor who owned it. It had been his mother's and he was planning to bulldoze and burn it that summer.

George and I talked with Paul, simply saying that we wanted to construct a small building and asked if we could buy the wood or if he would let us have it if we tore the house down for him. He agreed to let us tear it down and the work began. Later he simply gave us all the materials we had salvaged. A plaque at Catherine House notes our deep gratitude for this special gift from him and his wife, Alice.

We were delighted to find tongue and groove knotty pine under the siding. Those boards form the comforting inside walls of Catherine House. We salvaged windows and fireplace bricks and spent several weeks with the help of friends dismantling, hauling various materials home and removing nails. It was a far bigger project than we had anticipated, but we weren't deterred. We had sand moved from one spot on our land to the poplar grove to build up the ground for proper drainage. By August, we were ready to lay the foundation. Hugh came to help when the concrete was poured. His wife, Mary, was also there. She told me long afterward that she hadn't believed we could get a cement truck way back there and had doubts about Catherine House ever becoming a reality. I had never doubted. Maybe I was too naive to take any obstacles seriously. However, I also realize that I have long adhered to the philosophy: **"See what needs to be done, do it, then ask if it's possible."** As far as I was concerned, this was God's project. If it was meant to be built then and there, it would be.

A poem from *Walking on Water* by Sister Maura SSND speaks to my belief.

Autobiography

Let my life go - in the will of God - this way.
Let it affirm the impossible.
For the impossible is evident everywhere.
Little can be proven absolute from day to day.

4

But there are: faith, love, prayer.
Indomitable frailties that phoenix
Before and while and after I say amen.

After the foundation was set we plunged into the actual building: one room plus a small screened-in porch to ward off mosquitoes. We were well on our way by mid-September.

How fondly I remember that long, warm autumn. Christopher, four, was our only child not yet in school. Almost every day until the end of October he and I trudged back and forth, red wagon in tow loaded with hammers, nails, saws, stain, varnish; whatever the day's work required.

Boards were cut at the garage by power or handsaw. Roof boards were pieced together to make the required length, then fit in place like a giant jigsaw puzzle. Since George and I had helped roof our own house under the leadership of our friend, Denis, topping that little building was a cinch.

Tom and Maribel remodeled their upstairs that summer and gave us leftover oak floorboards recycled from another building. Tom built a banquette, a 2'x6' bed that sits low to the floor-perfect for our needs. Others donated doors, screens for the porch, a wood stove, a table and chair, and a porta-potty. The total cost of construction was less than $600 including insulation in the walls, ceiling and floor.

In December the wood stove was installed. We were finished enough by then to have our dedication service. Buddy and Jean came from their Mt. Hope Community in northern Midland County. Their community had donated a door and the stove. Buddy led the singing. Len and Micky shared prayer and scripture. Over thirty people crowded into that little space, asking the Holy Spirit to bless this house, this Catherine House, and make it a holy place.

Twenty-five years later, Bob, who experienced many inspiring retreats at the Gethsemani Monastery where Thomas Merton had lived, said that, for him, Catherine House was an even holier place.

There is deep significance for me in the gift of that old ramshackle house, taken apart and crafted into something entirely new. It speaks of the transformation that has gradually taken place in me as I have opened my mind and heart to silence, to prayer, to God's transforming love.

So much enthusiasm had carried us along. I was certain we would have a steady stream of pilgrims once the door opened, but that first year hardly anyone came. Many people talked about it: those who had helped build it, those who had heard about it. Getting away to a quiet place from the distractions of phone, meetings, people and events sounded enticing. (And there was no charge for using it.) But actually making time to go away to an isolated hut with no electricity or running water to be alone with God was another matter entirely. After checking it out, one woman frankly said she didn't know how she would get along without a TV.

It was humbling, frustrating and disappointing that people didn't flock to this prayer house in the midst of their modern 20th Century lives in order to embrace an ancient idea. Part of me could understand that attitude completely. I had grown up in a large family on a farm lush with people and activities. A desert experience was totally foreign, both geographically and spiritually.

I tried to be patient, giving a tour when people came to visit, hoping it would catch on. At one point I shared my frustration with Catherine Doherty at Madonna House. She cautioned me to be patient, to **"Let God take care of bringing who He wishes to use it."**

Growing up as a Catholic, the very thought of sitting alone with God in silence was strange to me as well unless it was in the few minutes of my morning or evening prayers or when as a young adult, I slipped into the Chapel at Aquinas College between classes. Even then, the brief outer silence was filled with inner prayers for others or myself. The concept of silently listening to God, of just sitting with God simply to sit with God, had neither been taught nor modeled. Yet that mysterious possibility had spoken to my heart in northern Ontario, far from my roots in Shelby, Michigan, and had put down its own roots 120 miles due East of that home-farm, with the deep knowing that this was an idea, and an experience to be shared.

However, despite few visitors to Catherine House, life continued to be full and rich with a young family, with involvement at St. Brigid Church and School plus connections to local and state peace activities. The years flew by.

Catherine's words proved true, and in time the Holy Spirit has inspired hundreds of visits to this little desert nestled in what has become a lush, wooded area.

We usually refer to Catherine House as a prayer house, though in a guest book entry John referred to it this way: **"I'm taking the hut with me wherever I go."** We say prayer house rather than a poustinia as the latter implies the presence of a poustiniki who is available for spiritual direction. Even though I was a spiritual director for 10 years and sometimes met there with people, and even though our friend, Bob, often ministered to his directees there, its use was not envisioned in that capacity. The original vision of it being used only as a one-on-one with God was altered as well.

We also realized that the Madonna House practice of a 24-hour stay in total silence with only a loaf of bread, a jug of water and the Bible wasn't practical for most people. Some came for one hour, some for several. Occasionally guests stayed for a night or more. We simply welcomed all who came.

Eight years after opening the door, that steady stream we were hoping for was at least at the trickle stage. The numbers have waxed and waned over 36 years, drawing neighbors as well as guests, some who have traveled hours to get here. Some, like Nan, have become dear friends who have blessed our lives in special ways. A few guests have come only once, to look, to pray or to go home and create a prayer room or space of their own.

Glimpses of Guests

Mark was our first long-term guest. He spent five days. **"I have entered into this retreat attempting to be open to God's will and grace. I pray that I grow in faith and faithfulness during this time. I also pray to grow in courage and humility."**

Peace-activist priest/friend, Peter, made several yearly retreats, spending a week or more at a time. He greatly enjoyed lying on the ground gazing at the stars, a view he couldn't have in the city. Some guests come with a jug of coffee or a book. Peter came with a Coleman stove and enough canned food for the duration. He usually stayed put, coming to our house only occasionally for a shower or to use the phone. His entry: **"These 12 days of solitude have been already a noticeable blessing. Deep shifting within and new attentiveness without. A deepened commitment to the oneness of all things."**

Those who love to be out in Mother Nature are always richly blessed just to be here. Etta made several visits, and one time she even walked several miles from her city home out here for a retreat. One of her guest book entries reads: **"The wind was my companion and light today."** Linda drove up from Ann Arbor, also grateful to be out in the country: **"Nature is my temple and my solitude."**

Our son, Matt, spent a night there and was filled with thoughts of loved ones who had died, gratitude for ones still with him and anticipation of the birth of his first nephew: **"Bob, Helen, Dick Darger, Emily, Grandpa and Grandma, Papa and Nanny, Uncle, gratitude for family and friends, anticipation of Chris and Jennifer's son."**

Our daughter Ann Marie's guest book entry read: **"Thank you for such a beautiful and peaceful place."**

My sister Cris and nephew Dan came for **"A brief but wonderful visit."**

When Sister Rosalee journeyed from Detroit and spent several days, she drove into Midland each morning to attend mass. She also cooked in our kitchen once or twice, the only guest who has done this. Ordinarily they are expected to be self-sufficient. New ones first stop at the house to say hello. Regulars often simply come and go. We know they are here because their name is on the prayer house calendar and there's an extra car in the drive. They might honk in farewell as they leave.

I have come home on occasion to find notes, little gifts or money left on the kitchen table or hung on the back door. Such gestures are appreciated and the money was used to buy wood. One year we re-stained and replaced screens with Tom's generous donation. However, we make it clear that donations are never expected or required. This house was built as a community effort for the use of anyone who is drawn to come. It is a mutual ministry. When people express their gratitude I always thank them in return. Anyone who seeks out this sacred space will be abundantly blessed by presence and prayers of earlier visitors.

Over the years a number of people have come with a friend, a spouse, and occasionally in small groups, such as our prayer group, local members of the Baha'i faith community or of the Lay Cistercians. Groups of youth, from a church or an organization, have also come to walk the path and visit the prayer house. George spoke about Thomas Merton to Catalina, Aimee, John and others of a faith group. Along with thank yous about the prayer house, Donna's comment added: **"Your love and enthusiasm for Merton is obvious."**

The largest group gathered in 2011 as part of a reunion. This was the Farmer family, descendants of one of the first African American families in Midland that lived in our home in the late 19th/early 20th Century. Several generations came from Michigan, California, Pennsylvania, Nevada, Canada, Ohio, far too many to fit into the prayer house together so they lined the path as they waited to enter and to sign the guest book. I have delightful memories of a slow-winding train of bright umbrellas moving under a warm rain. I still feel the grace of their presence on this land.

Sometimes mothers and grandmothers have brought youngsters. When Chris came as a toddler with Kelly she penned: **"Christopher's first visit with Mom!"** When he was 23, Chris came briefly and left a drawing of his hand as if it was signing the guest book. No words needed.

Clara and Emily came with grandma Marlene and left this message. **"We came to visit your prayer house and to visit God."** Another granddaughter, Mary, 7, wrote: **"I like your prayer house."**

Our granddaughter Chloe, first visited Catherine House as a toddler. When she was 5, after helping me clean, she drew a picture of herself sweeping. When she was 6 she drew a picture of God that now hangs above the holy books on the desk. A few steps from the prayer house is a simple labyrinth of flat stones with a chair in the center. Chloe has walked it many times. I told her that when she sits in the chair, she is sitting in God's lap. She seems comfortable there.

All seasons of the year are lovely in their special way. Our daughter-in-law, Jennifer, chose fall to bring her mother and her friend, Sinead to come have a look.

Most visitors to Catherine House call or email to set up a time to come. Occasionally neighbors or guests of neighbors walk over to our land and slip in and out without our knowing it unless they sign the guest book. In June of 1983, Anonymous left this message: **"A very peaceful and quiet place where one can be alone with the Lord. I thank you for your trust in people."** Another entry: **"Thanks for a place of peace. It's good you have trust in people and us. I hope people don't wreck it. It is a nice peaceful place."** Yet another note from a mystery guest: **"This is a cool place for you dudes to build. I hope no one trashes on it because it was a good idea."**

Our oldest son, Peter, left this message: **"Jesus be with me through the struggle within."** When our youngest son, Christopher was 12 he wrote: **"When I'm at the prayer house I don't feel scared, but I do feel secure and calm. I feel at ease and at home. It's not a place to fool around in but a place for thinking and praying. I like it also because it's so small and cozy."**

It pleases me that other kids have also left cherished entries. At age five, on a visit with her grandmother, Peg, Paige wrote: **"I like to visit the prayer house."** Neighbors Shelby and Sammy came to peek and pray and wrote: **"Love this house."** and **"I love God so much."** When Grandma Debbie brought

Sophie and Garrett, Sophie drew a picture while Garrett penned: **"Thank you for letting us pray in the prayer house."**

The door is never locked and a sign on the door reads: **"Visitors to Catherine House, you are welcome here. This is a holy place. Please use it accordingly."**

Precious Gifts

I approach the poustinia on a path that meanders through scenery that is lovely in all seasons. As I round the last gentle curve there it is, like an old friend, waiting to gather me in. In the spring and early summer Honeysuckle, Autumn Olive and wildflowers enhance the beauty of the walk. Before the trees encroached on the once open land, I walked through a sea of Goldenrod and Queen Anne's Lace.

When we first built Catherine House we trudged through tall grass. That was ok in dry weather, though if I headed back on a dewy morning or after a rain, even wearing a slicker and high rubber boots, I invariably arrived at the door with soggy knees.

Then one summer our next-door neighbor, Don, asked permission to mow a path so his family could ride three-wheelers from their land onto ours. When I told him later how much I appreciated it as a dry route to Catherine House, he was pleased that he had inadvertently obliged us. He kept it mowed for many years. When he and Ginny sold their house, we joked with them that part of the final deal should include that the next owners would keep up the path. That's just what happened! Our new neighbor gifted us for the next 20 years. A sign now designates it as **"Tom's Path."** He never said that he spent time in the prayer house, but often said that the mowing itself was a very calming experience. Even in the winter the path is usually easy to walk. RVs have never been a problem, the neighbors are very considerate and guests are left undisturbed.

So there it stands, waiting. I enter through the screened porch where a sign identifies it as Catherine House with Shalom written beneath it, along with the framed message relating its history. I step inside and see two windows bordered by faded yellow curtains, one facing east to catch the morning sun. A table/desk holds the guest book, a candle, a picture of Catherine Doherty and several holy books.

Initially there was only a Bible, a gift from Ted and Jean, and a few Christian prayer books. That collection grew after the terrorist attacks on the US on 9/11/2001, when we invited people from all faith communities to donate copies of their holy books. We now have a large assortment, including the Koran and The Book of Mormon along with Jewish, Hindu, Buddhist and Baha'i prayers. One friend stopped spending time there after seeing the Koran. However, when our Muslim friends, Shona, Ray and their son Zak came, their message in the guest book read: **"Oh God, you are the source of peace."**

One wall holds a cruciform from Assisi, Italy: Jesus hanging on a rough slab of wood. A picture of a copper statue of Our Lady of Combermere that stands in the yard at Madonna House hangs over the desk. These were gifts from Harry and from Bob and Dee. A Native American symbol given by a Viet Nam veteran in memory of his friend blesses another wall.

Under one window is the banquette, a nice place to rest. A sturdy oak rocker waits near the stove. It invites me to sit, and I do. A glance takes it all in. Nothing is hidden, a reminder of how I should come before God - open and available, as transparent as the windowpanes.

13

Transition Moments

When I enter for a retreat, one of the first things I do is bow to Mother Mary, then to Jesus. Next I prostrate myself beneath the cruciform, then turn on my back with my arms outstretched and say, **"Yes, Lord."** Usually I do this in a normal voice, but depending on the degree of confidence and commitment I feel at the moment, I might shout or chant it. Occasionally I whisper it, hoping God isn't listening too carefully.

I do this prostration and recommitment for two reasons. First, for the sense of humility it inspires. It also takes me back to the first time I did this at Madonna House's Cana Colony where we went as a family in the summer of 1982.

Near Lake Madawaska, not far from Madonna House proper, is where families can go to relax and to renew their Christian life. George and I had talked for years about going as a family. Finally, the summer after we built Catherine House, it happened. At Cana, families stay for a week in simple cabins, or in tents or campers. Through recreation, daily mass, conferences with a Madonna House priest and other staff members, and sharing a kitchen, families are invited to deepen their love for Christ.

One night that first week I was praying alone in the chapel of Our Lady of the Lake. Suddenly I had the urge to prostrate myself before the Blessed Sacrament. I had never had this prompting before - in plain truth I thought that people who did it were a bit weird.

I sat there awhile hoping "it" would just go away and leave me alone. It didn't. I almost got up and left, but something told me that I must do this or miss a most important chance to let the Holy Spirit work in my life in a new and deeper way.

I didn't want to appear foolish. What if someone walked in while I was down there? I almost chickened out but finally did it. With my face on the floorboards, my first prayer was that no one would come near the chapel for the next few seconds. That's all the longer I intended to stay.

There. I could get up. But then I felt a prompting to turn over onto my back. Talk about feeling vulnerable! I hesitated then figured I'd come this far and might as well see it through. I rolled over, still desperately hoping that no one came anywhere near those doors. Responding once again to the gentle but persistent promptings of the Holy Spirit, I said, **"Yes, Lord."** then scooted out the door, much relieved. It was done. Yet at the same time I knew I had committed my life to God in a deeper way than ever before and that something significant had just begun. The mystery of that brief ritual and of those few words touches me each time I have renewed this commitment during the 32 retreats I have made at Catherine House. After this sacred ritual I might spend time in silent reflection or in reading scripture. I'd like to be able to say I do fully-focused meditating, and I have on rare occasions, but my highly active mind keeps inviting me to go here and there and I often succumb, enticed by reminders of meetings, family needs and other responsibilities that I had intended to leave outside the door or give over to God. I take solace in St. Teresa of Avila's belief that if she spent an hour or two in prayer and was restless and distracted the entire time, God still accepts the effort gratefully.

In early years, visits to Catherine House usually consisted of 20 minutes of silent sitting. During retreats, I might sing or dance. I'd often take a nap, go for a walk, read a spiritual book or a novel, or sit quietly attempting to minimize my own activity so God's activity could be maximized. Once I just paced the floor, back and forth, back and forth, trying to work free of some burden. A guestbook entry from Diane could have been my own. **"Is this a prayer house or a dumping station? As I walked down the path this morning a burden pressing me down, tears already blurring my vision, throat tightening...I began to absorb the calmness of this hallowed ground and noticed the pines and the dried weeds holding their share of snow. They don't have to carry more than they can carry. I don't either. I loosen my hold on this problem, Lord. It slips from my grasp and is dumped at your feet. You are the LIGHT of the world. Alleluia."**

When I can hand my world and the entire world over to God, who is my Light I come away not with my life magically back into right order, but with more strength, tolerance, patience or whatever is needed to continue to live day to day in a more loving mode.

There is a blessed relief in silence. Not just that silence of no TV or radio, or the absence of other clatter and clutter of life. I've never been one to watch much TV and can go for hours with no radio or CD player for entertainment. But the silence I've discovered at Catherine House not only relieves, it refreshes, renews and offers perspective and direction. Nan C. Merrill captures it well in *Psalms for Praying*: **"Listen long in the silence that the Word may be heard, that decisions arrive from the depth of your inner being where wisdom dwells."**

Over the years I grew to desire this silence more often than my once-a-week on a Thursday afternoon. I needed to nurture myself so when the kids came home from school I could be more present to them. I needed it when they were hurting or made bad choices, and I wanted to help them through a difficult time. I needed it when George and I saw an important situation from entirely different perspectives or when someone outside the family needed help and my emotional and physical energy was at low tide.

Now that our four precious kids are grown and gone and the house is very often quiet with just George, me and our dog, Jazzy, in residence, I am still walking that path regularly, seeking the silence as preparation for what each day may bring. If I can absorb and embrace it, I make better choices. It would be foolish to attempt to make a weeklong car trip and think that filling the gas tank once was enough. It's just as foolish for me to travel through an entire week of living while thinking that one fueling of my spiritual tank will suffice. A guest book entry by Bob said it well: **"The journey forward to God is successful only if we keep coming back, daily, hourly, by minute, second or at each breath."**

Author Paul Claudel speaks of the importance of silence in our journey with God. **"To hear the voice of the Word, we must know how to listen to His silence and above all, to learn it ourselves."**

Hearing the Silence of God

In that wilderness of northern Ontario at Madonna House I first consciously heard the silence of God. But God's silence doesn't reside only in a secluded, faraway place, or in a church, temple or mosque near home. It resides in me. Having a special place to get away from my usual routine is a pure gift. I am ever-grateful for this building, nestled on the back of our land, that offers a quiet space in a world that is often noisy and that sometimes seems to be spinning out of control. Being here has helped me discover the secret room Jesus spoke of where God will reward us with God's self if we go there in faith. But that room is not in a building. It's in my heart. I'm learning how to enter it at any time or in any place I choose. Sometimes it is reflected in my poetry. Catherine Doherty would say I'm beginning to create a poustinia in my heart.

Empty Room

Sitting in Poustinia
Quiet, empty, still
No books calling
No phone ringing
Empty room filled with God
Empty me filled with cobwebs
Empty yet full
I open my heart
Love overflows

Catherine House has become a way to discover an empty room for pilgrims who come to meet God in this out-of the-way place. They step into silence and are blessed. Then they step back out to be a blessing to countless others.

There are hundreds of recorded visits, many by one-time visitors. Some guests will fill a page, quoting scripture and recording insights gained or burdens lightened. Marge, our most regular guest, often writes one-liners: **"Praise for the beauty of creation." "Gloria, Gloria, Gloria in Excelsis Deo."** Or simply **"Alleluia!"**

More Glimpses of Guests

One winter in the early years before our neighbor had obliged us with a real path, a friend was coming to spend the night. George went back to haul up the porta-potty which needed emptying. He didn't remember it could be taken apart, allowing for much lighter, easier transport, so he hauled the entire unit to the house on a toboggan. I hauled it back later after a storm, wading through snow up to my knees.

I moaned and groaned on the way, angry with George, wondering why we got ourselves into this ministry in the first place. But, as always, it was worth it all because it was fruitful for others. After his stay, Jon, who lives in the city, wrote: **"This day of peace and stillness has been a gift in my life. May His peace grow in us next year."**

The next visitor was my husband, George, in mid-January. **"When you stand too close to a painting the image becomes blurred. You have to step away in order to see the painting more clearly! Today has been a day of standing back in order to see more completely."**

Over the years more people have ventured out during the winter to sit in the rocker by the fire. One February, A.J. drove up from his Catholic Worker House in Detroit, two and one-half hours away. His entry read: **"What a wonderful rest I've had here. Grace has poured out of this place and into my soul. Thank you, Lord, for the nourishment and fidelity. Help me to tend the coals of your love within me. Grant peace to all who follow."**

The fact that the weather was so cold that his car died and needed to be jumped before he could head back to the city was not recorded. But his soul had been warmed by his visit and he planned to come again.

George or I will go back and start a fire for guests so the prayer house will be toasty on arrival. Occasionally people have insisted on building their own. I used to say that starting the fire was part of my job description. I'm often glad that I have let guests do it themselves, as it has been enlightening.

Diane came often for a number of months before moving to Brazil: **"My first fire in the stove. How many times, Lord, have you tried to kindle the fire in my heart? These brother logs yield their stored energy that they have held onto. They let go of this form of life in order to warm my feet and fingers. In the face of such sacrifice the best I can do is to give God praise, to use this warmth and my life to give glory and praise to Him."**

More of Diane's entries helped me realize how clearly God speaks through the ordinary if our hearts are open: **"Today the fire wouldn't start. Then I remembered TWIGS! 'Don't scorn the small things.' Lord, if I could act as a small twig to carry the fire of your love to the people who are great logs, I would be very privileged and blessed indeed. Your warm love is constant. Alleluia. Blow on the coals of my heart, Lord."**

Joan looked forward to her prayer house visits on Friday mornings. When someone suggested they spend that time with her, she kindly but firmly refused. For her right then it was important to go to Catherine House alone. Later she did bring her daughter, Rachel. One of her entries reads: **"With the coming of winter, the prayer house again draws close around the fire. No more days reflecting on the porch under poplars. I, too, draw close to the fire searching for warmth as cold winds blow through the door cracks. Dear God, cold winds blow through my spirit also today - fears, concerns, worries - help me to draw closer to your power and to be able to open to your strength."**

Judy has come in all seasons and always experiences Catherine House as a **"Sacred place."** A different Judy shared this about her visit: **"Enjoyed a lovely walk to the Prayer House and the variety of flowers that greet you along the path…I was looking forward to walking the labyrinth to experience the path first hand…was in awe by the beauty of all of the birch trees and the peacefulness that surrounds this Prayer House."**

After a brief visit, my sister Karen penned, **"Thank you Lord for the gift of life and the gift of family. How blessed I am."** At another time, her daughter Denise came, and when another daughter Cheri and family visited us, her husband Bryan referred to Catherine House as **"a very special place."**

Ellen spent **"A beautiful afternoon in this wonderful quiet space."** Jenn thought of it as a **"Spiritual Oasis."** Lauren, another young woman noted that **"Peace lives here."**

Ronnie, who had supported us in building Catherine House, had thought for years about coming but figured she would need three days there just to slow down enough to sit quietly for a while. She eventually came, returned quite often and discovered that time away from her many community involvements was a blessing: **"Profound peace as I seek the will of God! Help me to love deeper and have more compassion. God's mercy encompass me. It's Lent but I feel like singing alleluia."**

Seasons of Change

Seasons. My life has been full of them, seasons of mothering, of marriage, of my growth in faith, of undertaking new projects and relationships. Some I have moved slowly into and through. At other times it seems as if I have raced through

21

the entire spectrum from spring to winter. The grace with which I maneuver increasingly depends on the amount of silence I make space for in my soul and how open I am to God's embrace.

My concept of God does not include arms, but, just as I told my granddaughter, Chloe, that she can sit in God's lap in the center of the labyrinth, I am comforted by these soothing parenting images that come to mind: **"You cradle me in your arms as I once cradled my own little ones. Let me draw strength from your great love. Let me become still and quiet within as I am touched by your calmness. Praise You, Creator God."**

Calmness within is reflected in outer calmness. Rushing through my days can be a signal for needed change. When I collide with myself when turning a corner, I know I'm in overdrive again. It's time to pull off the expressway and traverse a quiet country road. Going to Catherine House or even just being close to it helps me slow down and refocus.

This change of pace was a relief back in the 80s, akin to the euphoria of first love. It all sounded exciting, this going off to a secluded hut. For a short while I thought I was still in charge, but the veneer was thin. I would go to the prayer house taking spiritual books, devouring them so I could learn more about God. My plan was to finally read the Bible from cover to cover. I went with prayers of petition for others and myself. I spent a great portion of the time talking to God, stating what I wanted in my life and asking that it be granted.

Sometimes I would trudge back to Catherine House totally defeated, seeking relief from a particular situation. In the early years my visits were often sporadic and always with the hope that I would get something or that God would fix things for me. That original idea of sitting in silence with God had gotten lost in my help-me-first-God focus.

In retrospect, maybe I referred to Catherine House as a little desert then, but I really used it as a recycling station. I wanted to be relieved, refreshed and renewed without being involved in the hard work of transformation, then go back into the world and ramp up speed again.

This change of pace made sense on some level, but doing what needed to be done and often taking the lead was in my DNA. I had always basically been a confident, competent person but found myself wondering where I was headed. I tried to listen but didn't get clarity. Was I going to regain a sense of direction and decisiveness? After months of dis-ease I journaled: **"Lord, here I sit in a muddlepuddle. When I make a decision about all this it will be not with my head alone but with my head in my heart. Then I will move on in integrity...I want to get my mind off myself. I realize that this is what stands in the way of following Christ, but I've done it this way so long that I'm in a rut and fear the new way, fear for myself and for what it will demand of me: the giving up, the turning from seeking my own comfort above all else. The temptation in seeking to get my mind off myself is to get busy again with outside things, to throw myself into something. At the same time I hear this call to get away from self-absorption, to less busyness, to more listening. That doesn't seem to fit with taking on more activities. So it seems I must just discipline myself to focus on you and not myself."**

Gradually I began to reap abundant blessings by slowing down and reordering priorities. But the flip side of the coin was loneliness. Stepping off the merry-go-round threw my inner life into chaos. Where some things had once been clear and in order, much was nebulous. I was addicted to rushing and busyness. My self-image was closely bound up with that, which is why slowing down and dropping out was acutely painful. I felt cut off from many people. I questioned my worth. I was terribly lonely for some time.

Outcomes of Changing Pace

When George and I were first involved in peace issues we went to conferences, sometimes taking the kids. We gave talks about families, peacemaking and living a simple lifestyle. During the Call to Action years when the Catholic bishops called the laity to more involvement in the church, our activities continued as we helped form a local Pax Christi group. Even though I greatly enjoyed being involved in outreach activities, much of my prayers and journaling at that point revolved around the idea of slowing down. Once again poetry captured what was in my heart and handed it back with clarity.

Remembering

Lord, slow me down.
Let me respond to your call,
To come aside for a while and rest.
Teach me to be still and quiet within.
Slow me down, Lord.
Remind me to sit at your feet often
So I can listen to your voice,
Hearing again and again the truths of old,
Lest I forget to remember.

As I slowed down, what surfaced was the idea of playing. Looking back I can see that the two unfolded hand in hand: **"Like a spring wound up tight and locked, I don't know what it means to be unwound. I unlocked the thing and somehow thought that the unlocking was the unwinding when that was only the releasing. Now comes the slow, slow unwinding, experiencing the pain and unfamiliarity as each section becomes more loose, less rigid, while traveling into unknown territory, an uneasiness of not being in control."**

The temptation was to pick up the pace again. But instead I made:

Snow Angels

It was just a snow angel.
Simple enough to create. Child's play.
Plop down in billowy, sun-sparkled snow,
Lay back, back, back,
Resting under the old maple tree
That had suddenly done a headstand,
Caught up in the spirit of fun.
Legs out, creating a flowing robe
In a single stroke.
Arms arching above my head
Angel wings magically appear.
I hoist myself upward,
Careful not to disturb
The wonder I have wrought,
Then quickly make a dozen more,
A host of angels singing in my heart.

Joy! Joy!
Memories flooding forth from childhood games
To meet and rediscover
That same child who lives again.

Simplicity. Unclutteredness. Snow Angels. I yearned to nurture the child within, to grow beyond my adult, rational, intellectual self to simplicity and childlikeness. I wanted to toss aside the what-ifs, the excuses, the tons of baggage that kept me weighted down.

In the busyness of raising a family and becoming involved and over-involved in church, school and peace activities, the goal of listening to God had definitely gotten lost. In retrospect I realize that much of the time I couldn't have heard if God had been "shouting" at me, and I suppose that often was the case. George Maloney, S.J. says in *Inward Stillness,* **"We can easily enough see where the fault lies in not praying more deeply. It is because we avoid turning deeply within ourselves and remaining in silence. Our fragmented, sinful nature does not like to live in silence because silence has a way of revealing ourselves honestly. We pray with distractions and without force because we are afraid to be ourselves. And we refuse to be ourselves by refusing to enter into silence in the depths of our hearts."**

The silence that once was soothing had become disturbing as it began to inch its way into my heart. I wasn't sure I really wanted to listen to God. It might require more than I was able (or willing) to undertake. Even years later, my journey reflected how much farther I needed to grow: **"Mother Mary, help me to be able to fill up with silence... at least my big toe. That would be a good start."**

Love or Obedience?

Obedience. I was hearing the word everywhere. In a homily Father Jim said that obedience is at the heart of Christ's relationship with God. When I told him I had never heard that message before, he said he had talked about it a number of times. He was our pastor for six years. I attended a conference around that time and the speaker said, **"Obedience is at the heart of Christ's relationship with God."** I always thought that love was the centerpiece.

Love was a word I could handle. It allowed me to insert my own definition. Obedience was a no-nonsense word that left no doubt about its meaning. It challenged me to sit up and pay attention. In truth it sent shock waves through me.

About this time someone suggested I read Henri Nouwen's *Making All Things New Again*. One paragraph brought clarity. **"...it is clear that we are usually surrounded by so much inner and outer noise that it is hard to truly hear our God speaking to us. We have often become deaf, unable to know when God calls us and unable to understand in which direction He calls us. Thus our lives have become absurd. In the word absurd we find the word surdus, which means deaf. A spiritual life requires discipline because we need to learn to listen to God who constantly speaks but whom we seldom hear. When, however, we learn to listen, our lives become obedient lives. The word obedient comes from the Latin word audire, which means listening."**

In the guest book I penned, **"Lord make my ears grow like Pinocchio's nose so I might hear more clearly and discern your will for me."**

I was in a crisis. I was beginning to get some discipline in my prayer life. I was praying quietly every morning for a few minutes. I had slowed down somewhat in my outer life. Would I be able to quiet the inner noise, the questions about my priorities, the resistance I felt about this business of obedience that wouldn't leave me alone? What other inner noise might I have to deal with if I just sat with God and tried to listen?

In spite of my fears and unease, I still continued to say **"Yes, Lord."** when prostrating myself. I was in full agreement with St. Peter's statement. **"To whom else would we go, Lord? You have the words of eternal life."** On reflection, those were probably the times when I whispered my assent, or said it in rueful resignation.

If I dug into the issue of obedience I would come smack up against the question of who was in control of my life. I had had a transition experience when I was 28 and had said the words to commit my life to God. Actually I later realized that what I had done was to invite God to be a special part of my life. God loved me. I loved God. It was easy to transfer my childhood belief that **"Jesus loves me"** to the love of an adult for a God who continued to be good and loving to me. That fit very easily into my spirituality. I could treat God as the honored guest, but I was still host of the party. I liked it that way. I felt secure thinking I was in control.

I returned to Madonna House in 1985 with my sister Joan. Father Sharkey, the chaplain from Aquinas who had taken me there in 1967, was then a member of the community. He lived in a poustinia for several days a week.

I shared with him that I had been hearing the phrase over and over again, **"Leaning on the everlasting arms."** He told me it was a call to contemplation – to more silence. He added that it is a difficult road but deeply rewarding. He also said that we're all called to be contemplatives, no matter what our vocation.

I sat with him that night and sobbed, knowing before that trip that tears would be shed – tears of release. I didn't know what would be released but was certain it would happen. Somehow that experience helped me to make this slow, painful transition from taking charge of my own life, from hanging on to my stubborn willfulness, to surrendering in obedience to God's will.

Catherine Doherty often said that we need to close the door of our intellect and open the door of our heart. **"Presuming, that is,"** she wryly added, **"that you have initially opened the door of your intellect."** I had opened it all right. I had my life and God pretty well figured out, thank you. I was grateful for God's help now and then as long as I called the shots. It was very rational. Much was subtle but was there just the same.

Those tears loosened something. Maybe that's the first time I began to trust God not in a childish but in a child-like way: to trust enough to begin to lean on those Everlasting Arms and, at least for a moment, not wonder what it would cost me.

God's Embrace

The following morning I awoke at dawn. A fire of joy burned within, beginning in the area of my heart and spreading outward and downward. I was very aware that it did not move to my head. My journal entry reads: 9/18/85 **"It was such a pleasant, reassuring experience that if it had color I would have glowed. Praise God for this confirmation that I am on the right path."**

Would saying yes to contemplation and silence turn me into a recluse? What about my responsibilities to my family and others? By now I had kids from elementary to high school ages. Would I become more self-focused? More solitude sounded so inviting, yet I didn't want to separate myself from others in negative ways. It was most helpful to learn that in the English language, solitude means "alone" but in Russian it means to be with everybody. One who prayerfully enters the desert doesn't leave the world behind but takes it along.

Slowly I gained clarity as to what I needed to see ABOUT the world in order to accomplish what I needed to do IN the world. I didn't have to save it. (I actually visualized taking the globe off my shoulders.) I needed to be part of changing it, trying to use my gifts and living in a way that might encourage others to live as Christ modeled. At the same time I needed to be journeying deeper into Christ myself. More silence and stillness seemed to be calling me. What would it require of me?

That call stretched back to my first desire to stay in that poustinia at Madonna House. It was building up in me, filling some of the empty space. I would draw on this resource over the years, often unknowingly. It had gotten muffled in the daily workings of life; completing a college degree, marriage, raising a family, becoming involved and over-involved in church, school and peace activities.

Some of the messages had gotten through of course. God doesn't wait for us to rest in the silence in order to get our attention, but speaks in many ways through the people and events smack in the midst of our noisy daily lives.

I had heard God speak through my children as I breastfed, rocked and sang to them, as I volunteered at school and watched them grow. I heard it through George's support and quiet spirit, through Pax Christi friends who were working to create a better, more peaceful world. I heard it clearly in our finding this old house with ten acres and a grove of poplar trees just waiting for a prayer house to be nestled there. It was present in the people who were coming to enter the desert both here and within their own hearts.

God's voice continues to speak through current activities and connections, through my grandchildren, Chloe, Easton and Dawson, daughters-in-law, Michele, and Jennifer, and my son-in-law, Guy, all who are so dear to my heart.

Nothing and Everything Would Change

For a while I approached this "more silence" hesitantly. Now I embrace it like an old friend. My life is both changed and unchanged. In her book *Poustinia*, Catherine Doherty addressed this, speaking to Madonna House lay apostolates living in an urban area who were starting to spend more time in silence while continuing their ministry. **"Nothing would change and everything would change. They would continue to be engaged in mazes of meetings, contacts, plunging ever deeper into the secular society. They would remain on the important but humdrum level of this strange apostolate of martyrdom and patience, dealing with migrant leagues, open housing, model cities and the rest but everything would be changed in depth."**

I deeply desired to open myself further, not just to more silence, but to the new growth it would generate in me. Once again poetry spoke the truth. I wrote it and then tried to live into it.

Transformation

Lord, burst me open like a pregnant seedpod.
Spill me out in abundance into the
Fertile soil of your love.
Take the weak seeds.
Nurture and caress them into
Unexpected beauties, late bloomers
Though they may be.
Take the strengths
And let them blossom gloriously
In the sunshine of your love,
In truth and grace and steadfastness,
So that whatever weather prevails
In my soul they will stand firm,
Bearing light and hope to all who pass by.

Results from opening myself more were three mission trips beginning in 2000, the first one was to the Dominican Republic to help in a school. The second was when our son Matt was in Guzman, Mexico as part of a volunteer program where he was a photographer for a newspaper. George and I visited him and we spent time in Guadalajara helping school children. I greatly enjoyed being with children and youth from cultures outside of the US. These experiences laid groundwork for my belief that we are all brothers and sisters, part of God's family. I still connect with Carmen de Jesus who was a teenager when I first met her in the DR. She is now a doctor, and it is a blessing to have this personal international connection. Then, the third trip was in 2006 when I went with Grand Rapids Dominican

Sisters to New Orleans in the aftermath of Hurricane Katrina. I have deep gratitude for being able to be there with Dominicans, who have a long history of standing up, speaking out and reaching out to do social justice and to help countless people in many ways. It was a privilege to be with them. Even though those three trips were each under two weeks, they broadened my perspective and helped prepare me for much later connections with others from different parts of the world.

Prudence, Passion, Prayer

When those three opportunities arose, I knew that saying yes was the right choice for me. Outreach opportunities are endless, locally, nationally and internationally. As I learn about other needs through friends and the media I often wish I could go help there and there and there. Yet at the same time I know that prudence must partner with passion and prayer to make the right choice at the right time.

Immersion in silence offers the possibility of discernment. The Holy Spirit calls me outward and inward: listening-discernment-decision-listening-discernment-decision. It's a continual process that is dependable and directive when I'm tempted to say yes to an invitation or to an inclination that is not my calling. Maybe earlier it was. Maybe later it will be, but now is the moment in which I'm living, and my body, mind and spirit know where I'm being led even in times of uncertainty. I'm learning to trust in the process as I journey deeper.

The depth has slowly increased for me decade by decade regarding my commitment to social justice, peace and nonviolence. In the 70s I was part of a group that gathered signatures on petitions calling for the abolition of nuclear weapons. I worked with related issues as well. In the mid-80s there was an effort in Michigan to close Wurtsmith Air Force Base in Oscoda where nuclear weapons were stored. A Faith and Resistance gathering was held at First United Methodist Church in Midland. That experience inspired me to "cross the line" at that base and risk being arrested. I discussed this at dinner with George and the kids. George supported me, and to my surprise and great joy, so did all the kids. Our high schoolers, Ann Marie and Peter, requested that I didn't let the newspaper write a story about me afterward. I agreed, and when approached for that story, I declined. Whenever I think back on that supportive moment I am richly blessed. Later I went to the School of the Americas, a combat training school for Latin American soldiers at Ft. Benning, Georgia, along with friends Frank, Evelyn, Jackie and Edith. Although I could have crossed another line and been arrested, I knew that was not what I was there for and chose to demonstrate my opposition in other ways. Over the years, when hearing about certain gatherings I was going to participate in, Ann Marie occasionally has teased me – though only partly in jest - **"Now, Mom, you aren't going to get arrested, are you?"**

Several activists, who were arrested and did jail or prison time for protesting the building of and threat to use nuclear weapons or who have worked for peace in other ways have blessed Catherine House and our land with their presence. Ardeth: **"Our time in prayer, reflection and sharing together is like yeast in dough, like nourishment in life, like light in darkness."** Carol: **"Grateful for another day to experience creation!"** Joni: **"Wonderful time away from the rat race."** Helen: **"Each time I come, I wonder why I don't come more often to this lovely spot of peace, quiet and prayerfulness."**

Goretti: **"The fire reminds me to be a warm person. Hopefully I can be back soon."** Liz: **"We spent a beautiful afternoon here at this marvelous place of God's presence and warmth. I do hope I can come back!"** Rosalie: **"...this holy stillness."** Mel: **"A blessed place to work, pray, and to co-create."**

Because I view the world from a global as well as a local/personal perspective, I know I'm called to reach out and to "be" out beyond my comfort zone. I spend a lot of time and energy working to be the change I believe I'm called to be. But as silence settles more deeply within so does the surety that this is my authentic path. I don't see my efforts as being an "apostolate of martyrdom", that phrase used by Catherine Doherty when speaking to those from Madonna House doing outreach ministries. I'm simply trying to follow my path. When invitations to stand up, speak out or "be" out arise, my RSVPs are decided by multiple factors: age, health, availability, family and financial circumstances, passion, intuition, spiritual direction and prayerful discernment. Sometimes it's an immediate knowing as a peace-filled yes or no arises. Other matters require a lengthy process, taking those same elements into consideration.

Knowing that I would not go to jail for the first offense of crossing the line, and discerning whether or not to cross another line and be arrested were fairly brief processes. Discerning whether or not to stay in the Catholic Church was a far longer deeper matter, one that did not surface until after 15 more years of growth.

Discernment - Future Decisions

As a life-long committed and deeply involved Catholic, the thought of leaving the church never seriously arose in 55+ years of membership. I didn't agree with everything the church did, but had high hopes as I participated in A Call to Action in the late 70s. I had no inkling back in the 80s and 90s that I would be dealing with this major fork-in-the-road question when the calendar changed to 2003. Far more immersion in silence would occur before that moment arrived and a four-year process would begin.

Meanwhile my busy life continued with regular retreats at Catherine House, some of which included Sister Teresita, my spiritual director for several years before she moved to Ohio.

It was good to recognize that even in my fast-paced life, for several years I had been able to slow down enough to make weekly visits, and that several days without agendas loaded with activities had become welcomed practices to which I looked forward.

I expect that God is calling the entire world to silence and solitude. Giving assent to that call doesn't have to take the form of going to a hut set apart in the country. For many people it's simply a call to create silent time right in their homes, work places or in their hearts.

Weaving silence into my days has been a step toward remembering who I am - a child of God, and also who God is - the Creator of life, the One in whom I live and move and have my being.

When I own this I can be more of the light I'm meant to be in the world. God has been called the Ground of our Being. When I am grounded in God I am not quite so easily tossed about by the forces that pull me first one way and then another, always with the possible outcome of distancing me from God and God's ways.

Precious Memories

Memories are so influential. In kindergarten I remember walking home from Blooming Valley country school, knowing Mom would be watching for me at the window. Some days I would be greeted by the mouth-watering fragrance of freshly baked bread, Long Johns and donuts. On winter evenings we played cards with Dad at the kitchen table. When I was very young he would play his harmonica, trot us kids on his knees while singing to us, or we would play around his chair as he sat reading or watching TV. I still feel the comfort of sitting with Mom on the couch enjoying the soothing sound of her voice as she read to us, or as she sang while working around the house. Picturing her in the living room teaching me to polka always brings a smile.

Sometimes I pull those precious old treasures out, letting them nurture me again and again. Even when I'm not conscious of them, they're still there buoying me up: **"Came back early this morning and spent an hour looking into the fire built partly with sticks from the farm in Shelby, partly with wood trimmed from our land: small branches that connect my beginnings with my continue-ings, consumed by the fire as I pray to be willing to let myself be consumed by God's love and more fully committed to living the Gospel."**

Silence is helping to build memories of a relationship with God that nurtures and sustains. Just as oodles of good childhood memories provide me with a sense of rootedness and security, so does building an adult conscious relationship with

God. It comes as I trust more to let myself glide deeper into life, to be renewed and refreshed in order to try to live a life more in line with God's kingdom. Trust and security increase as I move through my autumn years, and yet questions still remain.

Autumn Leaves

Leaves showering earthward
Autumn rainbows
Gliding into death
Graceful without a word of protest.
Would that I could die so gracefully
Die to selfishness, greed, vanity.
The key, I suppose, is
Letting go.
I thought I did that.
Another illusion?
Or have I just not learned
How to glide?

Stepping Back While Stepping Ahead

During the years when I was sure that I was the one in charge, I believed that I was doing God's work. The focus was more on me than on God. Now I have learned the illusion of that approach. By giving God the lead, I am much relieved that all the directing, planning and doing are not all up to me. When I listen carefully, direction, guidance and energy come. While I used to believe I had most of the answers, silence has left me with many, many more questions, and yet I feel more secure and peaceful than ever before.

"Experiencing silence and stillness is a good reminder that God is God and I am not, that I am to worship the Creator of the universe, not the false gods of ego, status, power, and greed of little value, yet with what great eagerness they are served." *The Imitation of Christ,* Thomas à Kempis

I am a list person, an organizer, a planner. I said to my daughter, **"I think I came out of the womb focused."** Following God's lead doesn't mean I have to let go of that. What I have learned is that THE LIST can become just the list. I'm no longer so driven to accomplish everything on it according to my way and time plan. I'm learning to let go of some things I can't ever seem to get to. When the newspapers pile up, recycling can be a wise choice. When it doesn't work to get together with an individual or attend a group gathering, maybe it's because it wasn't meant to happen.

In my 30s I often went to bed frustrated because of all the things I didn't get done during the day. In my 70s I have learned to be thankful for what was accomplished and not to fret too much about the rest. I sleep better now.

Falling in Love with God

Longevity and letting go have altered my perspective. I now understand that my real work is not being busy, even the busyness of doing good deeds. My real work, my first vocation, is falling in love with God who will show me the paths I am called to walk; the God who won't always give me the answers I want, but who is the answer. Poetry once again reminds me to put first things first.

November Call

November wind
Rattling my window panes,
Reminding me that death is ever near.
It's time to take stock,
To reevaluate,
To take needed measures
Before it's too late.
So I stuff bulbs underground,
Pack them down firm,
Rake leaves and throw them on the garden and
Call the plowman.
Then I sit in my chair by the fire,
Fold my hands, quiet my soul
And begin my real November work.

An old memory from a silent weekend at a retreat house comes to mind. I was sitting in the chapel and the image of an abyss surfaced. I was invited to jump in with holy abandon. Even though I could only see a deep darkness I knew it was not an abyss to be feared, but one offering new life if I had the courage to say yes. And I did.

Often when journaling at that point, I would receive a response that seemed to come through the grace of the Holy Spirit: **"When you agreed to go over the abyss you looked like an adult – but your heart, your child's heart is what allowed you to step into that water and enjoy that crazy, splashing, comic ride into the abyss. An adult would not have done that. There were too many 'good reasons' for not doing it.**

Something in you is growing back into a child and I am glad – glad for me and glad for you. You can rest more as a child – you will have more energy, more spontaneity – there will be more clarity in the sense of moving with your heart."

Advent was approaching. That, of course, led me to reflect on Mary and her choice to be child-like and trusting. She was stepping into her own abyss. Did she trust that it was going to be life-giving?

Mary

And God spoke to a young woman,
To a childlike faith,
Knowing the openness would be there.
God performed a miracle in Sarah, too.
She secretly laughed at the possibility
And was surprised by the truth.
But not Mary.
"Be it done unto me according to Thy will."
And Truth was born anew.

The Path Unfolds

Thank God that much of our positive transformation happens in child-sized, not childish, steps. Trust encourages us to continue on our path. I am a dearly beloved child of God who has become an adult in my spirituality through embracing the child-like, trusting faith with which I was born.

I discovered this truth as my children were no longer little, as my parenting entered a new phase. The foundation for

41

developing a child-like trust-filled faith was laid as I grew up on the farm in Shelby, Michigan, daughter of Paul Alan Lound and Anna Katherine Haviland Lound; sister of Paul Jr., Don, MaryAnn, Karen, Dick, Joan, Cris, Catherine, Sharon and Martin.

It gradually took shape and gained more substance during college and several trips to Catherine House over the years. I started going to the prayer house on an irregular basis when Christopher, our son who had helped me work on the prayer house, was in first grade. Both he and I were walking down new paths.

There I was, college educated with a degree in sociology, capable, well organized. The next logical step would be entering the job market. I was, after all, part of the first round of Baby Boomers. However, a career didn't hold much appeal. Oh, I considered it. I almost applied for work outside the home and could easily have stepped into a position that was open. I didn't choose to be a stay-at-home-Mom so I could be out of step with women my age who were setting the tone for the future. I chose it because for me it was intuitively right. I didn't want to miss that opportunity and have never regretted the decision that George and I made fairly early in our marriage, along with choosing to live simply.

As I pondered what the future might hold, Marge, the one who has come to Catherine House most often and who has been a precious gift in my life, suggested that in a few years I might be doing something totally different than I could imagine right then. I instantly knew the truth of that and tried to stay open, to discern God's will. Even in silence it isn't always easy. But if I don't take time for prayerful quiet each day, I can quickly literally forget who I am called to be, can easily fall into unloving behaviors: needless rushing about, trying to control others, being more concerned about paying bills than I am about honoring God through my daily habits of living. Failing to make time for regular quiet is like neglecting my back exercises. If I get lazy and skip a few days, the muscles that hold my frame in proper alignment become flabby and my body cries out in pain. If I ignore the signals, the pain becomes a major problem. Then, unless I visit my chiropractor and recommit to daily exercise, I'm headed for real trouble. In much the same way I can lose focus and find myself tripping down a side path on Thursday that I was determined to avoid on Tuesday.

Seven years after that releasing-the-tears-meeting with Fr. Sharkey at Madonna House and after reading more about the call to contemplative prayer, I took the plunge. 1992: **"I'm on my way, off on a journey with St. Ignatius."**

Taking Time/Making Time

Making an Ignatian retreat can be a 30-day process, but Marge stretched it out to several months during which I met with her weekly, practiced contemplative prayer, did reflection and journaled. The leisurely process of those exercises formed my commitment to regular contemplation. I did the required 20 minutes plus 10 of intercessions for others. After almost a decade of faithful practice, shortly after 9/11/2001, I heard author Marianne Williamson suggest that people double however much time they already spent in daily prayer because the world surely needed this. I instantly said, **"I'll do it."** I went from 30 minutes of total prayer to one hour of contemplation, doing intercessory prayer at a later point in my day. Generally I do this five days a week, giving myself one day off and leaving Sunday as church-day.

It was comforting to know that I wasn't a pioneer in this business of moving more deeply into God. Countless others have gone before me. John of the Cross said: **"The Father uttered one Word. That Word is His son and He utters Him forever in silence and in silence the soul has to hear it."**

Knowledge of those early pilgrims helped strengthen my commitment and also buoyed me up as I journeyed. There was one who I was particularly mindful of as I sought courage to take more than hesitant baby steps into this silence. Who better to help me than Mary, **"a woman wrapped in silence"** as they say at Madonna House.

Being born into Catholicism in the forties, I grew up with Mary but never felt close to her. As a child I sometimes resented her when my playtime was interrupted when Mom called us in from the yard or home from the neighbors to say the rosary. I always disliked that interruption, and was grateful that she didn't embarrass us by shouting out, **"Kids, it's time to say the rosary!"** But we knew exactly why she called if it was after supper but too soon for bed. I would dash across the road, saying I'd be right back hoping no one would ask why we made a hasty exit right in the middle of a ball game. Somehow I survived those frantic moments. Even while attending a Catholic college my acquaintance was slight. Mary seemed to slip out of vogue in the sixties and I neither noticed nor mourned the loss until I found myself in a Christian community named in her honor. I expect that she had a part in my going there. Now I often fall asleep praying the rosary and value her as a loving mother.

On one of my trips to Madonna House, I stood beside the newly installed, very tall, beautiful copper statue of Our Lady of Combermere. As she towered above me, I reached out and touched her and received a warm embrace in return. I can still feel it after all those years. I know that she joins me in contemplation.

Woman Wrapped in Silence

Gentle woman, Mother of Combermere,
I come to you, touched by your tenderness,
Drawn into the security of your embrace.
Whispers.
Quiet invitations spoken in my heart.
Love surrounds me, closing out the darkness.
I rest. Soothed. Calmed.
Then continue my journey.

My niece Sandy also has a soothing relationship with Mother Mary. During one of several visits to Catherine House she wrote: **"Today I prayed, 'Hail Holy Queen Mother of mercy and our life, our sweetness and our hope...' and I felt that holy sweetness caress my cheek."**

Risks and Assists Along the Way

Shortly after my Ignatian experience, I completed two years of formation to become a spiritual director. Our instructor, Sister Roberta, spoke often about the resistance we put up when we're on the verge of change, and about how important it is to get ourselves out of the way, i.e. to do our inner work, in order to be an instrument of grace for those seeking direction. A poem I had written long before that echoes her wisdom.

Self SELF

Self, SELF
Put it on a shelf way in the back
Behind a stack
Of musty old books
Smothered by cobwebs and mold.
Self, SELF
Stuff it in a bag with a great big gag
So it won't go spouting all kinds of craziness
Self, SELF
Cram it in a box with 81 locks
And throw away the keys
Please.

Notes from an early spiritual direction writing assignment in 1994 speaks of this time of transition. **"Through my Ignatian exercises I also realized more clearly than ever how my independence is both a blessing and a hindrance. I was able to name and face my fear of being vulnerable, both to God and to others, and to see that it's all one issue. This seems to be a time for risking further, shifting away from building my house on sand to moving to the solid rock of God. Maybe this lull I'm experiencing is partly due to the resistance we spoke of in an earlier class. I know that this shift calls not for clear-cut, self-directed strong headedness but for a mode of surrendering and letting myself be loved. I am unsettled and**

apprehensive even as I desire to let go." Sister Roberta commented: **"Because it is a risk."** I knew she was right.

Those risks, to do the Ignatian exercises and to later train to become a spiritual director, were well worth taking. Both deepened my relationship with God and my belief in the discernment process. I continued trying to follow the lead of the Holy Spirit through a truly enriching decade, then moved on from that ministry, though I value the practice so highly that I continue to receive direction myself.

My move was to a deeper commitment to nonviolence and peace that eventually included an entirely new volunteer outreach as a professionally trained mediator. This was clearly an indication of Marge's thoughts those many years before about entering into something I might not picture myself doing. Initial training was 40 hours offered through the State Court Administrative Office program. Even though I was trained to work with several types of cases, I have mainly mediated Friend of the Court cases, in Midland and elsewhere, facilitating custody issues and parenting-time, helping parents of minor children work out positive ways to establish and practice what's best for their children. In the future I hope at some point to facilitate Balanced and Restorative Justice mediation when youth and those they have harmed come face to face, along with the support of community members.

Mediation is a non-adversarial process as opposed to having solutions imposed by a judge or by another authority. The process can be a painful, angst-filled experience ending in no resolution. However, the vast majority of mediations are successful. When parents agree to mediation or are required to participate by a court order, often they are stepping into a way of communicating and resolving issues that is foreign to them, thus the need for an impartial mediator. The effort is always more than worth it when two people can come to a Memorandum of Understanding written in their own words that they sign and take home. Hopefully their next interchange will reflect a growing confidence in how to communicate better and positively resolve their conflicts. Often, after a two or three-hour process, an agreement to move ahead to something more hopeful is reached. At that point participants often ask me, **"And you volunteer to do this?"** I smile and say that I greatly enjoy this work and see it as a way of bringing hope to children and families.

The World Will be Saved by Beauty

Beauty is expressed in countless ways. Creating a culture of peace through daily thoughts, words and actions brings hope to our world. Just as parents say to their kids, **"The people you hang out with make a difference."** So, too, does this matter in our adult lives.

I met Marge in the early 70s and saw her occasionally for several years. Then, when she started coming to the prayer house, we became close friends. It's fascinating how someone enters our life at one point - a mere hint of a relationship that is meant to blossom years later. In 1998 – the Year of the Holy Spirit - Marge and I became Peace Partners, making a commitment to collaborate as "2x2" in efforts to help build a more peaceful world. In 2000 she and I and Pastor Kirk of Midland's Trinity Lutheran Church initiated the Midland Interfaith Council for Peace and Justice and worked together with many others from various faith communities to envision and carry out a local version of the ***"UN Decade for a Culture of Peace and Nonviolence for the Children of the World."***

With great support from Jack and Ralph, Editor and News Editor of the *Midland Daily News*, our group wrote forums or did interviews of Christians, Muslims and Jews. Other articles educated the community about topics such as: Water, Meaningful Work, Slowing Down, Quiet Listening and Reflection, Environmental Justice, Building a Nonviolent World for Children, Eliminating Nuclear Weapons, and A Culture of Peace.

In 2003, Marge and her husband, Dick, George and I initiated The Helen M. Casey Center for Nonviolence in honor of our long-time Midland friend and peace activist, who modeled the belief that **"There is no way to peace. Peace is the way."** Whether it was a clerk in the grocery store, or a fellow inmate in jails where she was incarcerated three times for actions calling for an end to nuclear weapons, Helen connected with people respectfully and positively. We wanted to honor her while she was living. She died in 2004, yet continues to mentor and inspire people in countless ways. One way is regarding the importance of building relationships: to strengthen and deepen the old ones and welcome and nurture the new, all the while focusing on building a more peaceful world through peaceful means for everyone.

Activities initiated by the Center included Mindfulness, Nonviolence Training, Simplicity, Planting a Peace Pole on our land where the Center was housed, Dialogue with Midland Muslims, an Artisans of Peace retreat led by Bishop Tom Gumbleton, Tax Day leafleting at the Midland Post Office, Understanding our Neighbors - Listening More and Judging Less, gatherings in front of US Representative Dave Camp's Midland Office to demonstrate against war, nuclear weapons and other issues, and the Great Silent Grandmothers' Gathering for Peace. We also fundraised for the Nonviolent Peaceforce, the international NGO that trains civilians to provide Unarmed Civilian Protection (UCP) for people in conflict zones.

We hosted Art in the Grove. Artists, authors, poets, photographers, musicians, singers, dancers, actors, and storytellers shared their talents over several years. Dostoyevsky said: **"The world will be saved by beauty."** These gatherings were held out in Mother Nature under lovely white pines in support of this belief. I strongly believe that if we choose to protect all that is beautiful - humans and all of Mother Nature - we will help to protect the world.

Preston and Betty shared their gifts of beauty through photography and storytelling. Afterward they visited Catherine House. Preston: **"What a great use of the land. It is for people and the health of the spirit. Thanks for having me here."** Betty: **"What a beautiful and peaceful place! I love the quiet and the sounds of nature all around. And I love the intimacy of this tiny prayer house. Today's experience was a blessing to my spirit."**

Nonviolent God

As my faith journey has deepened, my belief in a nonviolent God has deepened as well. I would not worship and commit my life to a violent Creator.

I penned in the guest book: **"Easter Sunday! Alleluia to our nonviolent God who came to earth to live among us and to show us how to live nonviolently, to say no to the idol of warships, to unjust authority, to the habits of living that are not of God, to say yes to caring for the poor and for all our brothers and sisters all over the world. To say yes to risking our comfort, our reputations and even our lives as we make**

the efforts to follow the Way taught and modeled by Jesus, the incarnation of our nonviolent God."

To honor God, not only do I need to spend time in silent listening prayer, but also in nonviolent action to help create a more loving, compassionate world. Both are vital ways to give honor, thanks and praise to our Creator. For me, this little desert in the heart of the U.S. Midwest is a key player in this focus. The focus for others is as varied and nuanced as are those who seek to hear and heed the Holy Spirit. Amazingly, the desert can be fertile in all locales, in all seasons.

When we held gatherings in our Helen M. Casey Center for Nonviolence, guests might walk back to Catherine House afterward and leave a message. After leading a discussion about *The Anatomy of Peace*, John headed back on the path: **"On a day when peace was spoken of as a practical thing to do, beyond a theory, ways to make a heart at peace real, a way of being. To future visitors: May you find peace here."** Mary left this message: **"Lovely afternoon spent learning about alternatives to war. I leave filled with hope!"**

Sri Lankan students from Midland's Northwood University spoke at the Center during a fundraiser for the Nonviolent Peaceforce. NP had accepted its first invitation from citizens' groups in their country and had been there since 2003. Several years later its work was completed with many success stories to its credit, due in part to having trained local people to work with NP to end the fear-induced silence. At the end of their sharing that day, Dilan visited Catherine House: **"Found another place in the world that anyone can say is peaceful."** Sudha also shared his thoughts: **"May the wind carry the message of peace today. Praise the Lord."** At Northwood, housing was shared by students from families from both sides

of the civil war that had raged in their country for 25 years –
longer than they had been alive.

In 2011 when I suggested that instead of just having
fundraisers for NP, that we consider starting our own Midland
chapter, Mary, a high-energy, passionate woman was the first
to jump on board. Six years later her enthusiasm is even
greater in support of NP's efforts to **"Transform the World's
Response to Conflict."**

In late 2016 I knew it was time to let go of some efforts
in order to better focus my energy and time in fewer areas. The
decision was made by the board of the Helen Casey Center:
Marge, George, Norb (who joined us after Dick's death) and
myself, to close with a retreat celebration. I knew that Helen
would support this decision, because by stepping out of the
Center, I was stepping more fully into the Nonviolent
Peaceforce, by continuing to raise awareness of and support for
NP's international work as well as to continue our local
chapter's work teaching conflict resolution in area schools.

To Leave or Not to Leave

Changes are constants in our lives. Some of course are
risky and can be unnerving and frightening.

However, in 2003 I was neither unnerved nor frightened
when I realized that the question of whether or not to stay in
the Catholic Church was surfacing within me and was pressing
to be answered. When I first looked squarely at that question, I
knew that the element of risk was there. However, it was the
deep feeling of calm and peacefulness throughout the next two
years of discernment that both fed me and reminded me that I
am God's beloved precious daughter, and I would remain so no

matter where I chose to worship. Because public worship and building community with those with whom I pray are vital to me, wherever the journey led, it would definitely include participating in a faith community.

Shortly after posing the query: **"Will I remain in the Catholic Church?"** I invited four women to pray for me and to ask hard questions. And they did. Both my former and current spiritual directors were in that group along with two long-time Catholic women-friends. Responding to their many questions was challenging and clarifying. Others, both male and female, also shared their concerns and their points of disagreement:

1. **"What about the sacraments? How can you not receive them?"**
2. **"How can you consider leaving when so many others are hanging in there and working for change?"**
3. **"Is this a matter of Satan tempting you?"**

Such questions were not always comfortable but they were always helpful. My responses were of this nature:

"I have received the sacraments for decades. Now I will try to live into them more fully."

"Yes, people I admire and respect are staying in the church, but I have to do what I know I need to do."

"Maybe you're right and this is a temptation, but my heart doesn't tell me that."

I listened to anyone who approached me, including someone who challenged me for several hours, someone I dearly love who was deeply disappointed in me for even considering leaving the church.

Obviously this was not an immediate-knowing decision. I set myself a two-year period so as to be sure to allow time for prayer, retreats, listening and spiritual direction. Near the end a friend asked, **"If you already know what your decision is going to be, why not make it right now?"** I replied that even at the last minute, the Holy Spirit could make clear to me an answer opposite to what I was leaning toward. I wanted to remain open to that possibility. Maybe it would turn out that only the discernment process was what I had needed to experience. I was willing to wait and see, to be vulnerable enough to accept what emerged, even at the last nanosecond.

When my chosen date arrived, I knew I would leave. In September 2005 I wrote to the four women who had faithfully walked with me: **"After two years of discernment...I have left the Catholic Church. I leave in peace, with a deep sense of freedom and renewed commitment to my journey into God and in trying to live the Gospel as I am called to live it. I'm deeply grateful to each and all of you for everything you have been for me during this process."**

George had already left the church so I didn't need to explain to him. To our kids I wrote: **"I leave in peace, with a deep sense of freedom and with renewed commitment to my journey into God and in trying to live the Gospel as I'm called to live it."**

To my siblings: **"I did not leave because George left. It's an entirely separate matter...maybe this decision leaves some of you angry...That is understandable, but this is what sets right in my heart. I ask that you trust my decision and honor my striving to be true to my own faith journey."**

To my prayer group: "**Maybe this decision leaves some of you angry or disappointed. That is understandable, but this is what sets right in my heart. Two very significant positive signs to me have been that: I do not stand in judgment of those who remain in the church, nor do I desire that anyone else leave because I have done so. I ask that you trust my decision and honor my striving to be faithful to my own faith journey.**"

Why Did I leave?

Why did I leave the Catholic Church that I was born into and that I loved and was so deeply involved with for so long? A pivotal question: "**Are the structural practices and the center of power of the church oriented towards life? I no longer believe that it is. I believe there is something seriously off balance and unhealthy in its structure and power center.**"

A priest friend emailed me saying that those who leave are disloyal to Christ. Later he wrote again to explain what he meant. "**It is because I believe the church is the body of Christ in our midst...the broken body of Christ...always has been broken...I am often ashamed of the suffering we inflict on the church and the scandal we give to innocents. The past few years have been awfully painful for me as a priest and as a male. You have done lots of good...I would like to persuade you to stay with us as I would try to advise a youngster, just because his parents are an embarrassment, not to leave home.**"

It was not a fitting analogy. My dilemma was not on the level of embarrassment. Nor was I at an adolescent level of rebellion regarding church membership. I could feel his deep pain and didn't question his sincerity. I had known, loved and respected him for over 30 years.

In the early 1960s Vatican II proclaimed that the church is the people. I believed that in a very hopeful way and continued to believe it for decades.

Clearly there has been much good done by both clergy and lay people throughout the church's history.

For years I remained hopeful and focused on the goodness and deep commitment of the people as we participated in parish councils, ministered to the poor and to others, held positions on decision-making boards and were visible and vocal in the sanctuary as readers, cantors and Eucharistic ministers. It was becoming a far more pro-life church in the sense of valuing all who were involved and the gifts everyone brought to the community.

After faithfully participating for decades, by 2000 I no longer believed that the hierarchy was going to let go of entrenched attitudes and beliefs about where the wisdom resides, where and how the Holy Spirit moves, and who can be trusted with discerning what is moral and what is not.

Without a doubt, Pope Francis is making a determined effort to demonstrate caring about the wellbeing of those who are the church. His 2016 statement that **"the church must say it's sorry to LGBTQ people"** is a very positive sign. I believe this should be said to family members as well who were, in effect, forced to reject and/or too harshly judge their children or their siblings, causing deep pain for everyone. Francis also stated that apologies must also be said **"to the poor and to mistreated women"** among others.

Something else he said deepens and broadens the definition of what it truly means to be pro-life: **"We bring about the rebirth of Cain in every act of violence and in every war. All**

of us!...let us all become, in every place, men and women of reconciliation and peace!"

I have been asked since Pope Francis was chosen, might I return to the church. Even though I admire some things he has said and done, there is no desire to return.

Tipping Points

The initial questioning began and continued over many years as issues arose. I will focus on three that coalesced as tipping points for me, 40 years after the opening of Vatican II.

My decision was not on three separate issues, but on three tied together which I saw as examples of the lack of respect for and of valuing individuals of all ages, faiths and cultures, and of what power a few males in leadership positions have insisted was God-given to them alone.

The issues are birth control and the way it was handled, sexual abuse plus the cover-up and overall handling, and the document *Dominus Jesus* that addresses salvation of non-Christians.

The first, the handling of the Birth Control Commission in the 1960s requires a fairly lengthy, historical explanation. It speaks very clearly of what looked like the possibility of opening doors to trust in the laity and in the church's Primacy of Conscience doctrine, followed by the slamming of those doors, all in a brief period of time. This action, to me, speaks clearly of the fear that resided – and maybe still does – deeply within the power structure of the church.

I deal with the last two very briefly as, to me, the depravity of wisdom and of loving as Jesus calls us to love are abundantly clear.

Robert McClory's book *Turning Point* is about the two years of experience as part of the birth control commission from the perspective of Pat and Patty Crowley. They were appointed to be part of it by Pope John XXIII. He died in the midst of the Council and was replaced by Paul VI. Originally the commission was to be an all-male group, but ended up consisting of 58 members from all parts of the world including married couples, physicians and psychologists.

I read *Turning Point* shortly after its 1995 publication. It was disturbing to learn how the outcome of that commission demonstrated that papal authority and the actions of a few clerics made it clear, despite positive words and hopeful signs, that the voices and the witness of strongly-committed Catholic couples were dismissed by the Pope and a few clergy who were determined to maintain the status quo. Debates featured issues such as natural law, the limits of church authority and what constitutes intrinsic evil. Views ranged from Father Bernard Haring's belief of exceptions regarding birth control for specific circumstances, to Father Marcelino Zalba's belief that no exceptions to the law were to be tolerated.

Pat and Patty Crowley, 51 and 53, parents of five and heads of the Christian Family Movement (CFM) that attracted large Catholic families, served on the Papal Commission from 1964-1966. CFM members were not Church fallen-aways, lukewarm parishioners or cafeteria Catholics who accepted what pleased them and rejected the rest. Rather, they were the couples who took religion and their vocations as parents seriously enough to meet with like-minded friends at least every other week to discuss their faith and its implications in their lives. They were often in the super-active minority in their parishes, the ones priests and nuns depended on to hold everything together and to "pay the bills".

Part of the Crowley's contribution came from statements they had gathered from couples in the US and Canada from whom they learned about difficulties with the rhythm method and about widespread frustration over the church's ban on contraception. What did it mean, the Crowleys wondered, that this nucleus had been quietly growing frustrated - even hostile - at what they regarded as an unreasonable burden?

Collective views of six exceptionally active Chicago area CFMers, stated: **"We believe the end of marriage, considered in its natural as well as sacramental aspects, is both personal and social...The bearing and raising of children are normally the means by which this end is reached; the intention of fruitfulness is normally part of the marriage union. The number of children by which a couple can best reach this end can be determined...should be determined by the couple alone; if the decision is made to limit the number of children, this should be done on the basis of Christian charity i.e., unselfishly, out of a love that sees some larger good to be accomplished by the limitation. Discussions of the morality of sex in marriage should be based on considerations such as these, not on analysis of the isolated act of intercourse."**

Patty Crowley wondered: **"Does God really demand this (birth control) of people who are trying to live a full generous Christian life?"**

The Crowley's report to the assembly of bishops and cardinals, that included Fathers Joseph Fuchs, Michael Labourdette, Bernard Haring, Marcelino Zalba, and Jan Visser as well as Cardinal Leo Suenens and Archbishop Leo Binz along with many other clerics and moral theologians, was received by many with **"'extraordinary respect'...It was not definitive, yet for some it seemed closer to (Cardinal) Newman's notion of** 'consulting the faithful' than anything they had heard at the session."

McClory made it clear early on that going into this discussion, **"Marcelino Zalba, a Spanish Jesuit and recognized expert on Church authority, especially regarding family limitation, viewed the proposed change with undisguised horror - as if the very pillars of creation would topple. Patty Crowley, an American woman, wife, mother and organizer, saw the change as obvious and necessary, as self-evident as the Church's need to learn from its mistakes such as the condemnation of Galileo, the Crusades, the Inquisitions, selling of indulgences and the failure to take any clear stand against human slavery for nineteen hundred years."**

However, as matters progressed, struggles between the conservative and liberal theologians increased. Conservatives added Fathers John Ford and Ermenegildo Lio to the roster, but when the lay people suggested adding Fathers Karl Rahner and Robert Drinan as supporters, they received no response. As the Crowleys and other couples gained a deeper understanding of how church authority plays out, they wondered if change was even possible.

The 1930 previous encyclical on marriage, Pius XI's Casti Cannubii, stated that acts of artificial contraception are and always will be **"intrinsically evil,"** always against nature's laws and therefore must be strictly forbidden to married couples no matter what their circumstances. In 1951, Pius XII permitted the practice of the rhythm method for couples who had morally valid reasons for avoiding procreation. The official teaching at the time of the Vatican Council was Casti Cannubii. However, in 1965 the enlarged commission saw how the church had changed in its approach to sex, marriage and procreation. Casti Connubii could be reformed and everyone began to question the benefits of the rhythm method. **"And,"** said Fr. Henri de Riedmatten, **"the theologians had voted overwhelmingly that contraception was not intrinsically evil and the vast majority of the commission was now in full agreement that the church ought to change its ban on contraception while upholding overall the procreative purposes of marriage."**

Wisdom of Ordinary Catholics

De Riedmatten also reminded the cardinals and bishops how the Vatican council had extolled the **"witness of the faithful - the ability of ordinary Christians directed by the Holy Spirit to perceive what is true and what isn't. No longer appropriate was Pius X's distinction between the church that teaches and the church that listens: especially in discerning the morality of contraception, married couples ought to be among the teachers."**

As the consensus moved toward listening to the wisdom of the lay people like the Crowleys, Bishop Carlo Colombo warned that if the church backtracked on contraception this would **"endanger the very indefectibility of the church, the teacher of truth in these things which pertain to salvation."**

Father Zalba added, **"What then, with the millions we have sent to hell if these norms are not valid?"**

Patty Crowley responded: **"Father Zalba, do you really believe God has carried out all of your orders?"** She continued, **"On behalf of women in general, I plead that the male church carefully consider the plight of at least one-half of its members, who are the real bearers of these burdens. Couples are generous. Christian couples want to have children. It is the very fruit of their love for each other. What is needed is to rid** ourselves of this negative outlook on psychological and spiritual values. Couples can be trusted. They will accept the progress of change, and they will have increased confidence in the Church as she helps them grow in love and demonstrates her trust and confidence in them."

The majority vote was for change. Conservative leaning Cardinal Shenan of Baltimore opted for change because he had listened to his parishioners: **"The church develops and the sensus fidelium** (sense of the faithful) **plays a big role in that development."** After two years of deliberation, the majority of the bishops and cardinals formally approved the majority report.

Bishop Claude Dupuy composed a document that introduced that report which was fully approved, and the work of the Papal Birth Control Commission ended.

The Crowleys left for home very hopeful, with faith in the process and the nearly unanimous outcome. Major change was coming. Or was it?

In the end, the people, including the women who filled half of the pews, were not listened to. Couples obviously were not to be given respect and to be trusted because a few of the power holders in the Church, including the Pope, could not demonstrate their trust and confidence in them.

Due to efforts by Bishop John Ford and three other theologians: Fathers Visser, de Lestapis and Zalba, the latter being the one who was concerned about the millions the church had already sent to hell, and the key decision by Paul VI himself, the majority report was rejected.

Author McClory wrote: **"According to Bernard Haring, Ermenegildo Lio admitted to associates that Pope Paul was at first favorably impressed with the Majority Report and was attracted by its conclusions, but after two meetings with**

Cardinal Ottaviani and Lio himself, the Pope realized his mistake and was 'reconverted'."

In his biography, *Paul VI: The First Modern Pope*, Peter Hebblewaite concluded that Cardinal Ottaviani and associates controlled the outcome. They believed **"...the whole experiment in consultation and letting non-professional theologians into the debate had already inflicted untold damage on the Church...No matter what the chapter on marriage in Gaudium et Spes** (Vatican II's document on the Church in the Modern World) **said, and even though it pointed clearly in the direction of 'responsible parenthood,' the Holy Office could (and did) reply that Gaudium et Spes is only a pastoral text while Casti Connubii is the milk of pure doctrine."**

A new encyclical Humanae Vitae, issued in 1968 rejected the commission's work. When the Crowleys were called by the Associated Press to get their reaction to the encyclical, they were stunned and asked themselves why they had ever gone to Rome in the first place.

Clergy Sexual Abuse and Denial

A second element that formed the tipping point was the clergy sexual abuse scandal.

Briefly, I have this to say about this unconscionable matter: For a church with a long history of claiming to honor, protect and value families while emphasizing in its formation of parents and children that clergy are to be trusted, to have perpetrated such crimes against the most vulnerable, and then, when exposed, to have handled it by cover-up, denial and the whisking away of people such as Cardinal Bernard Law into the safety of the Vatican, is an additional sinful abuse of children, of their families and of power.

Okay, so, it's a given that sinfulness exists in the church as a human institution. It's a given that sinfulness exists in the people in the pews and in those of the hierarchy. No discussion required. However, given that a key principle of the church is respecting and valuing life, was I willing to remain a member of a church that didn't truly value its members, either as children who would say, **"Yes, Father."** or as adults who would say, **"No, Father."**?

I agree with whoever said that the refusal to be honest and humble enough to name and condemn its own actions as clearly as it has named and condemned actions of its members for 2000 years is unconscionable.

Dominus Jesus

The document, Dominus Jesus, published in 2002, definitely was part of the tipping point in my decision to leave the Catholic Church. It was written by Karl Ratzinger, then head of the Congregation of the Doctrine of the Faith, and now retired Pope Benedict XIV. Having worked over the years with people from several Christian and other faith communities: Hindus, Muslims, Jews, Baha'i, Unitarian Universalist Fellowship through the Midland Interfaith Council for Peace and Justice, and through other organizations and efforts, I find it reprehensible and heretical given who Jesus is and what his life modeled, that the Catholic Church hierarchy would give any credence to support the concept that this large portion of God's children are in a **"gravely deficient situation"** regarding salvation.

I read every word of this lengthy document that uses complicated explanations in its attempt to make it sound reasonable and rational. I quote it only briefly because, to me, this one paragraph speaks clearly to the dysfunction of the hierarchical church.

Section VI - The Church and the other Religions in Relation to Salvation - paragraph 22:

"With the coming of the Savior Jesus Christ, God has willed that the Church founded by him be the instrument for the salvation of all humanity. This truth of faith does not lessen the sincere respect which the Church has for the religions of the world, but at the same time it rules out, in a radical way, that mentality of indifferentism characterized by a religious relativism which leads to the belief that one religion is as good as another. If it is true that the followers of other religions can receive divine grace, it is also certain that objectively speaking they are in a gravely deficient situation in comparison with those who, in the Church, have the fullness of the means of salvation."

Even if I hadn't had the privilege and blessing to know and to highly value people of various faith communities, I would have rejected a document that I see as unworthy of a church that claims to be the direct follower of Jesus Christ.

I could no longer give my heart to that church. I knew that something would die in me if I stayed. Someone challenged me, **"Isn't this like the question of leaving your country? You don't always agree with all the US government does, so are you going to leave the country?"** My simple answer was that my journey in faith is the most important journey and how, where and with whom I am connected has to set right in my mind/heart/body and soul.

Moving On

Madeleine L'Engle said, **"Do what you have to do until you know what you need to know."** I stayed in the church when I knew that was what I could do. When my knowing coalesced and resulted in a tipping point, I knew just as clearly that it was time to go.

I am not a make-do person, and when people asked why I couldn't stay and reform the church, I realized that my role in this situation was not to be a reformer. I hope that those who remain involved continue to work to bring about positive change.

"There's life where the river flows." From my perspective regarding these three issues, life was not flowing from the power center of the church regarding sexual abuse and cover up, or regarding birth control or statements about salvation. Without a doubt, it's a given that from countless lay people and clergy, life continues to flow abundantly. I hope that Pope Francis will facilitate ongoing, life-giving transformation.

I didn't leave seeking perfection elsewhere. I have lived long enough to realize that every faith community is flawed and falls short of the mark at times. I also realized that I would take my flawed sinfulness wherever I go. But the Catholic Church is not where I belong. This had become clear after those two years of discernment.

Taking Next Step - Opening Next Door

Seeking another home in which to worship and build community was next. As Reverend Mary Jo, my spiritual director, wisely reminded me: **"Leaving is one decision, going**

somewhere else is another." That discernment entailed two more years.

In choosing another faith community, I was drawn to smaller ones and checked out the Quakers and the Church of the Brethren. The latter is a congregation with more than a 300-year history and has been in Midland for over 75 years. Some people do not know it exists here, and some ask if it is a non-denominational church. Actually it is one of the original peace churches along with the Quakers and the Mennonites. After visiting several times over two years, I joined in 2007 and have never looked back.

I did not join primarily because it is a peace church. Key draws for me were its welcoming members, its motto of **"Continuing the work of Jesus: peacefully, simply, together."** and four other key elements, not necessarily in this order:

1. A simplicity of doctrine: No Creed but Christ
2. This tiny community's commitment to share a large portion of its limited budget in outreach
3. The visible presence of the towel and the water on the altar as a reminder that as followers of Christ we are to be about foot washing on a daily basis
4. An openness to recognize the importance of honoring giftedness over gender

The Church of the Brethren is a denomination that has its own struggles over issues such as homosexuality. It also has women pastors. Even though prior to joining I had no plans as to how I might be called to serve, I have been a deacon and have preached for several years. Both have been rich experiences.

I like the simplicity of the building, of the sanctuary, of the worship service, and of the fact that, even though there is organization on district and regional levels, the Church of the

Brethren is not top-heavy. The smallness of our congregation, presents a challenge, but members have pulled together and continue to create a life-giving community that focuses on outreach locally, nationally and internationally including the CROP Walk, Heifer International and the SERV Sale (all Brethren-initiates) and the Nonviolent Peaceforce in its efforts to **"Transform the world's response to conflict."**

When the last paid pastor left several years ago, Art, formerly a Baptist pastor, received Brethren training and filled that role. He served for ten years with no salary. He and his wife, Darlene have been very special blessings. After stepping down as pastor, Art still ministers as a Deacon, preaches often and continues to walk the Gospel talk, washing feet all along the way. We recently hired a part-time pastor and believe that other blessings will unfold.

I know I am in the faith community where I belong. It was a luxury to have had plenty of time to discern and to decide as I stood at that challenging fork in the road.

Life, of course, doesn't always allow for leisurely shifting and sorting before major changes occur.

Sharp Turns in the Road

In April 2008 life took a sharp turn when our son, Peter, at age 35, needed immediate surgery for a malignant brain tumor the size of an orange. He had symptoms indicating something was out of balance, but figured these were due to the stress involved regarding the business that he and his wife, Michele, had started. The shock and dread of hearing this news was unnerving to say the least. Prayer and presence to him and his family, that included five-year-old Chloe, became priority #1.

Before this, my morning meditation happened most often in a rocking chair in the bedroom or downstairs in the Lazy Boy while the house was quiet. But at that traumatic moment I intuitively knew I needed to head outdoors. Before going to the hospital, I would get up early for my prayer pilgrimage within the healing beauty of Mother Nature in which I would do walking meditation for 40 minutes then sit for 20 in the prayer house using **"Love"** as my mantra.

The guestbook recorded the change: **"I started walking-prayer early mornings back on the path and on Gilstad's land. It is soothing and helpful to be out in nature and the 'quiet' of birds singing. I can no longer sit for my entire contemplative prayer as I had done since 1992."**

Later I knew I needed to be outside for the entire time, so I would walk our simple labyrinth and sit in the chair in its center or nearby in another space. Being out in nature in all kinds of weather at various times of the day – most often early morning – hasn't always been easy, but it has invariably been healing and sustaining.

Shortly after this all-outdoors routine began, several yards off the path near Catherine House, I spotted something blue in a wildflower area. I was surprised because there had never been blue flowers there. Investigation turned up a small rosary hanging on a plant. The cross was missing. It had only a medal of Mary, the Mother of God. I asked recent guests if it was theirs, but it wasn't.

I kept that rosary, not trying to figure out why I had it, just knowing it was a precious gift to me at that moment. I prayed with it often for a couple years: **"This a.m. after my walking, I was warm enough to sit in the labyrinth for 20 minutes as the snow came oh, so gently down. The rosary I found hanging on a weed back here the spring that Peter had** his surgery has been with me these days. A blessed mystery-gift."

An extra comfort is knowing that even when mysterious gifts don't appear, that I am blessed in countless ways unaware. That rosary disappeared as mysteriously as it came. Eventually I stopped looking for it.

The journey continues and the mystery unfolds, not in my timing but in God's.

My Six Mothers

One can never have too many loving mothers. A few weeks after Peter's surgery my entry in the prayer house guest book read: **"Yesterday my dear friend, mentor, mother, Mary Morrison died. In the 25 years we were friends, she and I often sat together sharing meals, laughter and prayer. What a great loss. I loved her so dearly and know I was dearly loved by her as well."**

Months later I created a sacred space in her memory near the prayer house, the Mary Morrison Glade of Forgiveness. A narrow, winding entrance just off the main path leads me there. It's called a glade because the sun shines in and Mary's presence in my life brought much sunshine. It's a glade of forgiveness to connect with the gardens of forgiveness that were created after the 9/11 attacks on our country. Mary would have approved of this inclusion. Her daughters and a granddaughter were able to come one day to see and be in this sacred space. Then we walked to the prayer house where I reminded them again that their mom/grandma and dad/grandpa were there when the concrete floor was poured.

Their notes in the guest book read: **"Hi, Mom. So wonderful to finally be someplace you loved. We all miss you so much."** *S*haron **"A lovely rainy afternoon. Saw the Glade of Forgiveness and am with Mom."** Madonna **"Restful."** Mary and **"Grandma, I love and miss you so much."** Cerilia

In this deep loss of Mary, I still had Jesus' mother, Mary, to walk with me, to gather me to her bosom, wrapping me in the mantle of her love. She offers solace and protection as only a mother can. One of those surprises during that difficult time was that I understood why I had gained several other mothers early that year.

As January 2008 started, before we had any idea about Peter's tumor or that Mary would die, I kept getting inner nudges to name mothers in my life. I did nothing about it for a couple months, then eventually those who kept coming to mind, in addition to my birth mother who had died in 2006, were my maternal grandmother; Dipa Ma, a Hindu whose story I have read three times because it touched my heart so deeply; the Metta Buddha (the spirit of loving kindness), and Shivangani Baile, a Hindu friend who had died a few years before. So I moved with this idea. When the April shock came, I had a five-mothers-team to help me face the surprising and shocking ordeals of Peter's surgery and weeks later the death of Mary, who then became part of my mothering group. I trust they will always be with me.

Those mothers rest in my heart and in my daily prayer basket, reminding me of their constant love and support, not just for me but for George and all our family. Each brings healing and inspiration and is helping me grow more fully into my real self. Why these particular mothers when there are so many others I might have chosen? I have no idea. I simply accept them for the gifts that they are. On hearing about this naming of mothers, someone asked, **"Why not invite fathers?"** My answer, **"Because that's not what came to me to do."** If it does, I will say yes to that as well and no doubt I'll again be deeply grateful for that enlarged circle of caring.

Nine years after his surgery Peter is doing very well. Our family's huge gratitude for Dr. E. Malcolm Field will always rest deep in our hearts.

Mother God

Calling God Mother, Father, Creator, Higher Power, Allah or using any other name shouldn't be an attempt to fully define God. Instead, it can be a way humans are comfortable connecting with our Creator.

Gale recorded in the guest book while on a two-day retreat: **"Father/Mother/God and all other names by which you are known, I give thanks for my place in your creation….I am not just in this place, I have already become a part of this place; its peace is within me. I am one with all creation."**

In 1997, during that period when I would journal and occasionally receive responses, surely messages such as these were coming from a love that is both fathering and mothering: **"…I need you now to embark on this journey to the heart of a child – Catherine Doherty is right. 'It takes awesome courage to live out the heart of a child.' But children have a natural courage and willingness to step out and move from the heart. So you'll have what you need as you need it. It's a package deal. Become a child and receive the awesome power to live it out. It's inseparable. Can't you see that? It's pure gift, pure grace."** In that same message, during the time I was having fun wearing clown suits and sharing my joke -jar: **"Be a child again.**

Your clowning and your jokes are all important parts of this becoming a child. Bring more laughter into the world, more gaiety."

Healing was needed in order to become more fully that child. In 2009, one of my prayer house retreats involved listening to audiotapes of Joan Borysenko's *A Woman's Spiritual Retreat*. I was listening while walking by our white pines and was deeply touched by the beauty of the sun sparkling on the raindrops that clung to the needles. The focus was about a woman's life cycle: guardian and crone years. Since at that moment Joan was talking about stepping into a grove and was inviting listeners to visualize an older woman, I stepped into our White Pine Grove and pictured one of my six mothers, my maternal grandmother Anna. She was walking toward me holding a baby who I instantly knew was me. The question I was directed to ask myself was: What gift does this child have that I want to develop more in myself? I knew right away that it was JOY. I took baby-me from Grandma Haviland and held myself for a while, then handed me back, and their presence was gone.

Earlier that very day I had wondered if, back in 1946 when I was born, Grandma had held me with joy in her heart. Was she as excited about me as I was about Chloe, the only grandchild I had so far? When I was born, Grandma already had lots of grandchildren, and she didn't live near us so didn't see me often. I doubted I could have been as precious. It was a tearful-sad, then a tearful-healing moment for me.

A few days later before heading out for my morning pilgrimage, I woke from a dream in which the strongest message was: **"Life is in the struggle."** I walked around the prayer house on the south circling path, listening to a nudge that I was to move that way - an unusual way for me to approach Catherine House. That put me in direct line with the statue of Mother Mary and a nearby large pine tree covered with autumn leaves. A tiny pine nearby was also decorated. **"How fun,"** I thought, **"like a Christmas tree, a reminder that we bigger people can be models of fun for the little ones and about how vital is the sense of playfulness in a lighthearted way within the struggle of life."**

I remember that someone at Madonna House had said, **"The world calls us to pleasure. The Gospel calls us to joy."**

Another way the child in me was healed and enlivened was through being blessed with tiny teachers right when I needed them. When our own children, who were special teachers in their precious ways, were in their tween and teen stages, I babysat with my godson, Chris John, and later his brother, Brandon. A decade later granddaughter Chloe was born and eventually our grandson, Easton, then his brother, Dawson. I have done childcare with all of them, and my gratitude overflows for the pure joy of being with them and for the ways they have awakened and have re-enlivened the child in me. I've also learned that being precious to a grandmother's heart has nothing to do with the number of grandchildren in my life. Each is a priceless gift.

Time with grandkids is nurturing so I can go do the difficult work – in gratitude and with more energy, bringing balance as I work to do other things I'm called to do – in fulfilling my purpose in life.

There's Life Where the River Flows

Retreats. I've made many. Some at retreat houses, some in the home of one of my spiritual directors, most at Catherine House. My first one there was in 1995. Five of them were 24/7 experiences (at least two lasted 5-7 days) then I returned to our house at the end. George or the kids would come back for brief visits during those days. Later I made two-day retreats and even more recently have spent a day or partial days only. In deciding the length and framework of time spent there, I listen to my body/mind/spirit. There are no more sleepovers as the banquette can't compete with a comfortable bed that supports my back.

At one point I knew I needed to have a complete change of time/place/duration, a totally different experience. In 2010 a four-week retreat fell into place.

In *Kaleidoscope: The Way of Women*, author Helen Luke wrote: **"Blessed is she who gives herself to the journey."** A four-week retreat was the journey I needed to take next. It would not be a directed one and not at a retreat center. It had to be a resting and detaching retreat away, in solitude, in an unfamiliar place.

It was Helen Luke who introduced me to the meaningful image of **"There's life where the river flows."** However, I wasn't thinking about a river-retreat. The one familiar thing I dearly yearned for was to see/hear/feel the waves on my favorite Big Lake, Lake Michigan. A river wouldn't fit, or so I thought.

Water has long been important, symbolically and physically, on my spiritual journey. Decades ago at Lake Huron I lay in the water in a simple baptismal ritual, then snuggled myself in warm blankets and napped on the beach. One rainy summer day I invited the little neighbor girls, Sydnie, Sammy and Shelby, to join me outside in their yard. It was a moment of pure grace as we laughed and played in the drenching downpour. Another fond memory was being alone outside in our yard at midnight walking and dancing while the frogs quietly sang during a warm late-August rain.

I was born and raised near Lake Michigan, and often as an adult I have gone there to stroll the beach and wade in the water. I was sure that somewhere on that beautiful shoreline there was a cottage I could rent, where in the off-season I could walk the beach as if I owned it, the perfect setting for a lengthy retreat. I longed to hear and see the waves crashing on the shore, then later to walk in gray rainy weather and curl up again on the sand, lulled by gently lapping waves. There was a cottage available to me, but the rent was too high. I trusted that something would work, and it did, but not in line with what I thought was best.

Thanks to Brian and Margaret I spent those precious, sacred weeks on a stretch of the Manistee River that flowed so gently that I couldn't even hear it unless I sat quietly on the bank or floated down it past a protruding tree branch where the water rippled gently. On arrival, I knew right away that it was exactly where I belonged that May of 2010 - in a somewhat isolated setting, drenched in silence and solitude, where contact with others would mainly be limited to phone calls with George and the kids. On the second day there I penned in my journal: **"I will relax and enjoy the outer quiet and hopefully grow into more inner quiet as I am carried through each day by the beauty of this home and setting...in this Great Adventure."**

While there I re-read my pile of journals dating from 1974. My plan was to later offer them to my daughter. At one point I seriously thought of pitching the lot but in reading on I noted bits of wisdom quoted from authors like Madeleine L'Engle. I thought they might speak to Ann Marie's own life down the road, or at least help her understand more about why her mom is such an intense woman. In the 80s, when I was in my 40s, I had read a lot of L'Engle's books. *A Circle of Quiet* was particularly formative in my life: "'**Ontology. The word about the essence of things; the word about being.' I realize…that the essential reason I am here on a four-week retreat is to attempt to get back down to my essential self. To do that I need oodles of quiet."** From another page: **"When a child who has been conceived in love is born…the joy of that birth 'sings throughout the universe.' I am so deeply blessed that the births of all our children, Ann Marie, Peter, Matthew and Christopher, were joyfully sung throughout the universe and that the singing continues on and on in their lives and in ours."**

After George drove me to the cottage, daughter Ann Marie was my one other visitor during those secluded days when she came and stayed overnight for Mother's Day: **"It was a comfortable, comforting time to be together. I'm so grateful for her effort to come. We walked and we sat by the fire and prayed together. We danced a polka - my favorite dance - and laughed and had fun. I am richly blessed in her."**

During those weeks I often danced to Mozart or Wagner, or sang at the top of my lungs. I built jigsaw puzzles, enjoyed "Pancakes and Pavarotti" breakfasts and "Dinner and Dvorak" evenings. As I detoxed from busyness and distractions, Mother Nature gifted me with a light snowfall on May 8th, enough to make a snow angel. I napped in the hammock on sunny afternoons and read a pile of books, including a *Junie B* one that granddaughter Chloe had sent with me. I journaled and walked each day. In reading Clarissa Pinkola Estés, *The 10 Phases of a Woman's Life* I learned I was in the age 63-70 phase of **"Reflection-becoming the watchwoman, recasting all that one has learned, being whatever one has become."**

Helen Luke's book about the myths of women and about the river flowing within and without, was just the book I needed to read. I thought I had brought it along for an entirely different reason. I had found it during a brief stay at the Sisters of Mercy in Farmington, Michigan. My Dominican friend, Sister Goretti, was receiving the Michigan Pax Christi Purple Ribbon of Peace Award and I wanted to be with her to celebrate. Looking for something to read before bed, I picked a book at random from the library. Two chapters caught my interest: Laughter, and The Joy of the Fool.

Just prior to leaving for that celebration, I chose a prayer/blessing from a basket in Sister Goretti's home: **"May the blessings of humor and laughter grace all the days of your life. May you know the lighthearted freedom of one who is secure in God's love and your own place in God's work. May you be tickled and teased and attracted by a loving God who wants to play with you today. May the blessings of laughter be with you."** These words and Luke's book fit perfectly together.

Early on during my retreat, I penned in relation to that prayer/blessing: **"Part of my discernment here is to understand more clearly what is my place in God's work. I'm not working at this discernment so much as I am placing myself in a space and an atmosphere where clarity may come. Praise God that it is not another project with a due date."**

Other thoughts spoke of full acceptance of the mystery of how life unfolds: **"Here I am on the river, not on the Big Lake with the rush of the waves or with the waves quietly lapping on the shore, both of which have soothed and strengthened me over the years. THIS is where I'm supposed to be now, near a gently flowing river that at least right here is not even moving over stones to make it bubble and ripple. The strong, quiet, strength-filled river that flows clear, that is a home for fish and that nourishes much life, that curves and bends as life curves and bends, meandering along and around and among.**

78

May my life become such a river as I move through this current phase."

While there I collected pebbles, a decrepit cedar fence post and even some sand from the river. They are by the prayer house or on the path, blessed reminders of that rich experience.

As my retreat drew to a close, Helen Luke gifted me with another surprise when she wrote about the Jewish Passover and the importance of celebrating it ritually to make it real. **"We must eat the Passover meal, the symbol of the crossing over into a new way of life. We must eat it standing, as did the Israelites, in complete readiness to seize the moment."** Instantly I decided to create a Christian ritual as a closing celebration of my retreat, of stepping beyond it into newness. It would be simultaneously light-hearted and serious.

So the day before I left, I floated down the river a mile or so. What I ate while standing in the freezing water **"...in complete readiness to seize the moment was an ice cream sundae with chocolate syrup...then I crossed over to a new way of life"** and walked through the desert – a sandy path – back to the house.

It was time to head home. A note on my final hours there: **"Pavarotti, silence, reading. My last morning here. Sat in the river. Collected sand from it to take back to the prayer house/labyrinth/path. Danced to a Mozart Sonata of what this has meant to me and to all its meaning that I have no idea about yet. What a gift this has been."**

On the River Once Again

As I worked on writing this book a few years later, I was again in a home on a quiet river, thanks to the generosity of

Skip and Julia. Their offer of solitude in the midst both of outdoor and indoor beauty was gratefully accepted. I was blessed with that gift several times: **"Solitude and the river. I couldn't have planned it better myself. And today the water comes from the heavens as well. I stood for a while in this drenching June rain and was soothed and nourished."**

In Joan Chittister's book, *The Gift of Years*, she says that aging is **"...the moment of final and full transformation...I have become the fullness of myself, but only after I was able to put down the cosmetics of the self, like the titles, the privileged, the symbols and the signs of being something more than I was – and at the same time less than I was. A burden of these years is the possibility that I might stay more buried in my losses than aware of my gains. A blessing of these years is the transformation of the self to be at long last the self I have been becoming all my life - an oasis of serenity in a world gone sour on age, the very acme of life."**

Perhaps some of her serenity is related to her recognition that **"...the number of absolutes in my life is precipitously reduced. I'm less dogmatic now about the nature of God. I'm not as sure as I once was about what is gravely damning and what is not. Most important of all, I am happy to put that decision in the hands of the God whose nature seems far more compassionate now as I have gotten more compassionate myself...Our role now is to be what we have discovered about life."**

Creating Rituals

Rituals. Treasures to be practiced daily or rarely. One of mine includes my Mantle of Serenity. A few years ago I asked

Kathy, who had shared monthly prayer and reflection time, if she would come to Catherine House and help me don a mantle while reciting words from a ritual I would prepare. I was delighted when she agreed. She even offered me a lovely, lavender shawl. My first response was no thanks, that I would use a bright colored wrap, one I would wear later on a cool day, but the lavender shawl won out and the rightness of that gift still blesses me. It was raining as we walked to the prayer house. I was glad that Mother Nature provided this spiritual element. As it turned into a downpour, we stood on the porch and I sang:

It's beginning to rain, rain, rain, hear the voice of the Father.
He's saying who so ever will, come drink of this water.

He promised to pour his spirit out on his sons and his daughters.
If you're thirsty and dry, lift your hands to the sky.
It's beginning to rain.

I felt the loving spirits of my six mothers as I donned the mantle. Would the ritual create the serenity? Would simply seeing it each day as it hangs on the back of the bedroom door and recalling that lovely ritual transform me? From time to time I don it over my pajamas early in the morning. Wrinkle-faced, sleepy eyed with hair in disarray, I have to smile as I peek into the mirror and say three times, **"I am a serene, lovely laughing woman."**

How am I doing with this serenity business? Not too well some days. Another reality check, but it's a worthy effort, measured in minuscule particles of growth.

Ritual is simple to create. Transformation is an ongoing challenge.

The Two Halves of Life

Richard Rohr has written an inspiring book, *Falling Upward: Spirituality for the Two Halves of Life.* In reading and rereading it, a key discovery for me was that silence is integral to the second half of life. For me, one key reason is that it can help to pave the path to serenity. Being in a space that is absolutely silent, for me is calming and nurturing.

In 2011, during my 25th retreat at Catherine House, I had planned to stay for three days and stayed for five. I had been reading Rohr's book. My message in the guest book reads: **"This morning when I was walking early I was very aware of the music of the frogs. There were two distinct choruses: the peepers that were making all kinds of noises with varied tones and tunes and volumes. Then there were those who were chanting in beautiful soothing unison. As I walked the path, the peepers were on one side, the chanters on the other. They made me think about what I had just read in Rohr's book when he talked about how we first have to build our life's container: our identity, our work, our morals, etc. Then in our second half we examine what's in our container, sort it, add new things or strengthen the old. If we haven't built a solid container in the first half, we will struggle as we get older because a solid container provides for us a solid place on**

which to stand." The frogs' soothing song spoke strongly of peace and serenity and the second half of life.

I remember my elderly mother sitting in the rocker by the window watching cars and no doubt pondering her life while waiting for visits from family members. I wondered if her days were long, and if the quiet house was in any way a burden for her. Further reflection leads me to believe that the silence was likely a healing, soothing gift. Mom was a woman of deep faith and had suffered, faced and dealt with many challenges in her almost-93 years. Sitting in wordless prayer may not have been her practice, but surely she was gazing at God in her own way as she prayed the rosary, held her family deeply in her heart and asked God to bless us all.

For me, wordless prayer is a balm for my spirit in a noisy, frantic world. And I'm finally understanding why Fr. Thomas Keating points out that one session a day of contemplation is not sufficient. The first, he says, is for maintenance. A second session is for deep inner healing, which is why he refers to contemplation as **"Divine Therapy."**

On that four-week retreat several years ago I made that second-session commitment, and began ten minutes of evening contemplation. Often I would spend that time in the quiet deep breathing of mindfulness, relaxing my body and my entire being at the end of the day. At some point it got lost in the shuffle and I stopped. Now I'm back to doing it for 10 minutes each night.

Darkness and Light

Early fall, 2012 - 5:00 AM - I head out for meditation, following our path, cross to the neighbor's land and stand there gazing skyward. The Harvest Moon is a marshmallow. My heart is lifted by its simple beauty. One deer calls to another. The rosy eastern sky gradually lightens and brightens, doing its own walk until it catches the moon, surrounding it with pink clouds. I stand still, absorbing the beauty, knowing there is more to come, content with what is. Then I walk again while the moon and I play hide-and-seek.

Winter - 5:30am - The snow is so crunchy-loud that it becomes a distraction and frustration as I walk. I'd like to quit right there, halfway through my walking meditation. Instantly the thought comes, **"This is life. I can't quit in the middle and let the 'noise' hold sway and give in to my negative reactions."**

On another morning I lie down on the earth. Snow angel. Cloudy. No stars. Balmy weather for winter.

Spring - Predawn walk on a Saturday as I move through a gentle mist. On the neighbor's land I head towards a stately white pine, back myself up into its embrace and rest a bit, grateful for the lack of weekday-traffic hum, happy to hear the performance of the peepers' chorale, a sure sign of spring even though the weather doesn't fit the calendar. I glance up at the pine boughs swaying in the breeze – contemplation at its best.

Another time I sit in the labyrinth. Today there is no circle of quiet surrounding me. The bird sounds are raucous. The early morning traffic a quarter mile away invades my space, not like some mornings when I sit unaware of distance noises. Another time I round a corner in the path and am greeted by dozens of little white tutus on the plants as if mini-fairies had become still-life in the midst of their ballet.

Early June. Near the end of my walk I bow first to the statue of Mother Mary, then approach the simple path of the labyrinth, stepping slowly from flat stone to flat stone. Then I sit in the center on the wooden chair, patterned after those at Gethsemani Monastery. I rest there in the center, symbolic of my yearning to rest in my own center. The birches appear different against a gray sky than when it's blue. But the space offers the same solace and my gratitude overflows. The birds are singing outside of this quiet haven. Even the barking of a neighbor's dog does not disturb this holy ground. My heart quickens and expands at the pure simplicity of this gift. Would that I could rest in this reality more often, not only the reality of space apart, beautiful as it is, but the reality of God's love that permeates all of life. As I rewind along the path, I glance up at the prayer house, noting that the moss-covered roof needs replacing. This little building has offered shelter to body/mind/spirit, to me and to many others for decades.

In the 80s when I occasionally practiced contemplative prayer, there were times when I was lifted up in ecstasy - a precious gift that lifted me out of myself. Today, after a long-established practice, I am often distracted and clearly pedestrian, both when walking and sitting still.

However, countless blessings result due to this simple practice, both those that are welcomed and those that challenge painfully. My mantra **"Love"** helps keep me focused. Distractions help keep me humble. It's all part of my never-ending growing process. In July as I walked a winding path at an early moment of the day, the words to a 60's song surfaced and took over. **"It's summer time, summer time, sum, sum, summer time..."**. I pulled myself back to my mantra: **"Love. Love. Love."** **"It's summer time..."**. Months before I would have been frustrated. Now I smile in acceptance and walk on.

Something is Birthing Within Me

Early in 2015 I was sure this book was complete and had no idea there would be a whole other part waiting to happen that needed to be included.

June 2016. The older I get, the more I appreciate and welcome the deep mystery that is life.

Recently a friend asked if I do walking meditation so I can figure out things. My immediate response was, **"No. I do it so things can be figured out within me."** The more I step back while stepping onward in the path of my life, the more space is opened for the Holy Spirit to work in me. Then sometimes mystery unfolds in adventurous ways.

Early in 2014, Ruby, who I have known for many years, asked if I would consider applying for an International Rotary Peace Fellowship. This took me completely by surprise, both because I was unaware of this program and because I was approaching my 67th birthday. Ruby explained that it is a three-month Professional Development Certificate Program in Conflict Studies and Peace and is offered only at Chulalongkorn University in Bangkok, Thailand. She thought it would be a perfect fit for me, given my years of organizing, my involvement with groups and efforts that promote peace through nonviolence, my mediation background, and teaching conflict resolution to students.

Reflecting on that moment, I never even thought, **"Are you kidding? This is not for me at this time in my life!"** Instead, my response was **"I'll think about it."** Very shortly I became excited about the possibility and shared Ruby's invitation with my husband, George, who responded, **"Go for it! I wish I had that kind of opportunity."**

So, I thought, prayed, applied, and waited. Near the end of that lengthy waiting time, my friend, Marge and I were walking the path to the prayer house and she asked, **"What if you don't get accepted?"** Without hesitation I responded, **"If it's meant to happen it will. If it doesn't, there are lots of other things I want to do."** Experiencing that inner freedom was pure gift.

The excitement began when I learned in late October that I was accepted into the 2015 June-August program. My Bangkok Adventure was really going to happen! I was filled with gratitude to Ruby and to Rotary for this tremendous opportunity. I also was pleased to have seven months to prepare before catching a flight to Thailand.

Rotary International has both the three-month certificate and the two-year masters' programs. The aims are to empower the leaders of today, and strengthen the leaders of tomorrow. Hundreds have graduated from both. The certificate program was initiated for people already working in efforts of conflict resolution and peace. Its 10th anniversary was celebrated with the completion of my Class 19. Rotary's website reads: **"Rotary Peace Fellows are leaders who promote cooperation, peace and conflict resolution in their communities and around the world. Fellows are chosen for their ability to have a significant, positive impact on world peace throughout their careers."**

I have especially fond childhood memories of my mother singing at home. One song was *Far Away Places*. Her gentle, lovely voice would sing **"I'm going to China, or maybe Siam..."** And there I was as a senior citizen heading to that very place now known as Thailand. As a high school student I had entertained thoughts of becoming an interpreter and working in New York City for the UN and thus working with people from all over the world. My dream didn't include being a world traveler, but my Bangkok journal entry spoke of unexpected surprises that can arise as decades unfold: **"Just as Tolkien's Bilbo Baggins in _The Hobbit_ responded to the Tookishness within him by heading off to places far away from his beloved home in the Shire, I, too, have responded to something in me that yearns to connect with others around the world who are working to create a more peaceful world through peaceful conflict resolution."**

Before embarking on this trip I experienced a nesting-instinct just as before each of our four precious kids was born. I had this long to-do list and later realized that this was because something was birthing in me again. What a gift to have that insight! I told my kids that this would be my next growing-up phase.

My introduction to Bangkok included visiting the Grand Palace and other tourist sites in a largely Buddhist country: **"At the Temple of the Reclining Buddha I lit incense at George's request and left a flower on an altar near the Buddha. Since we have a statue of the Meta Buddha (the Buddha of loving kindness) in our yard, this was an especially meaningful experience."**

While on that day of touring I picked up several pebbles, some that are now at the prayer house or in the International Stone Wall on our land. It was a full day – exciting and exhausting, and I held up well. Michelle, in her 30s, noted that I was doing far better than some of the younger Peace Fellows. She asked how did I do it and laughed at my reply: **"It's post-menopausal zest!"** I hope that she experiences this when she's older.

The Joy of Being a Student Again

My good friend Eileen gave me a journal in which to record my Bangkok Adventure. Since kindergarten and continuing through some graduate classes, I have always enjoyed learning. This energy was very alive during each day of this experience: **"I'm just trying to take a day at a time – a moment at a time – to absorb the intense classroom work, to discover the many gifts of the 17 other Peace Fellows from many countries and cultures brought together in the mystery of God's love for humanity and God's challenge to us to create a better world."**

Learning modules were interesting and challenging during the 30-hour weeks in the classroom. Field trips that took us beyond Bangkok and outside of Thailand increased our awareness and inspired our commitment to helping create a more peaceful world through peaceful efforts:

-The Concepts and Values of Peace and Conflict Studies
-The Diagnosis and Analysis of Conflict
-Conflict Resolution Skills, Approaches and Strategies
-Field Study - Northern Thailand
-Conflict Transformation and Building a Sustainable Peace
-Field Study - Cambodia

Stepping Into Stillness

Shortly before I left home I read Pico Iyer's *The Art of Stillness-Adventures in Going Nowhere* and gave copies to each of my kids. Son Peter smiled and quipped, **"When are you ever**

still, Mom?" I smiled in return and reminded him about my morning meditation and also that a nap is often part of my day.

In this tiny book, Iyer, a world traveler/writer, shared his discovery of the gift of sitting in quiet prayer and reflection and how transformative it has been for him. One of his many insights includes, **"What we do inner-wise becomes what we birth outer-wise…"** While in Thailand it was vital for me to continue my meditative outdoor practice.

On arriving in Bangkok I wondered, **"Where will I find a quiet place to meditate in the midst of a bustling city?"** Then, early on, when I went from my 20th floor dorm room to the 5th floor in search of a microwave, I stepped onto a lovely patio where birds sang in blossoming trees and patches of grass beckoned me to go barefoot. Between mid-June and the end of August, it was just what I needed – a sustainable luxury space where I could literally step into stillness.

Gratitude

The 5th floor became a special space for other reasons, like Sunday night gatherings of Peace Fellows to share cultural music, dancing and laughter. I penned into my journal, **"I'm so glad that I can dance."** At 68 I was the oldest Peace Fellow up to that point. (I was "Mom" for several of the young men.) Many of the Fellows greatly enjoyed dancing, and I like to brag that I out-danced them all!

Back in the classroom we also shared cultural music or sometimes danced for a few minutes after lunch before settling down for the next learning session.

A special surprise was in store when presenter, Jan Sunoo, an expert in Alternative Dispute Resolution taught us. He is also a lover of music. He plays the ukulele and invited us to pick up one and learn to strum along. His song of welcome to our class was to the tune of Woodie Guthrie's *This Land is Your Land*. While there I learned to play a little and did write a couple songs, one that we sang (also to Guthrie's tune) as a goodbye to Jan and co-presenter Meas Savath from the Cambodian Center for Mediation. (Sawadeeka means hello and goodbye.)

Sawadeeka to Savath and Jan.
Thank you for teaching us all you can.
We all are wiser thanks to you.
We'll make this world a better place.
Negotiation that's interest-based.
Define the issues! E-VAL-U-ATE!
Over in Cambodia: "Let's save the trees."
Mediation we will do with ease.
To Europe, Asia, and Africa,
Back to Australia and North America.
We'll take you with us as we live our dreams.
We'll make this world a better place.

A journal entry: **"Classes today with presenters Dr. Tom Woodhouse from the UK University of Bradford and Irene Santiago from the Philippines who was key in organizing the 1995 fourth International Women's Summit. In her mid-seventies, she is a strong personality, seems unafraid to speak out to anyone and has provided leadership on various women's issues for 40 years. Irene shared that setting up the Summit was a huge challenge. The Chinese government did not want it to happen, refused to allow it in Beijing, and insisted it take place in a village an hour from the capital. But** the women were determined to hold it and 30,000 attended from around the world."

Other experiences were noted in my gratitude journal that daughter Ann Marie and her husband Guy sent with me:

"I'm grateful for one more day of learning with these people in this space in this place in the world."

"...for all those I love and for those I'm coming to love here in Thailand."

"I'm glad that I live in a country that has an elected government and not one under a military coup like Thailand has."

"...for all those who love and support me."

8/9 (Nagasaki 70th anniversary) "...that lots of people all over the world are working for peace through peaceful means."

"Today I joined Matt (Australia), Jerome (Sri Lanka), Flori (South Sudan) and Mediatrix (Kenya) for worship at a Catholic Church. It was interesting to see that Jesus on the cross hangs to one side near the front and a huge gold statue of him with his arms raised high is the centerpiece. Instead of doing handshakes of peace we did a wai (bow) to each other. One of the songs I liked was 'God is Good, All the Time'. Prior to arriving at the church, a woman approached Matt and said she was hungry. He took her to 7-Eleven and bought her food. I told him that my first memory of worshipping that morning would be of him living Christianity before he even entered the church."

One night I talked with Palestinian Peace Fellow Jamil. It was Eid, a Muslim holiday celebrating the end of Ramadan, and I wanted to give him a hug. He showed me some sweet and funny pictures of his 11-year old son. Jamil cried when he first saw them because his son said: **"There is no Eid because you are not here with us."** Jamil teaches nonviolent conflict resolution at Gaza University as part of being director of International Affairs there. He spoke about how Palestinians' lives are vulnerable and about how the ongoing violence at different points in their history has been so chaotic, and yet they keep on going. He values Rotary and what it is doing in the world and wants to engage it to work in Palestine. He knew that being in Bangkok then was right for him. Other Fellows like Jerome, Flori, Mustafa and Umar have also lived through much violence in their home countries. I greatly admire and am grateful for their passion for and commitment to helping build a better world through peaceful practices.

Oh, the Horrible Waste of War

Field trips transformed history from disturbing words on paper to heart-felt, deep sadness for what humans, all created by the same God and thus who are all brothers and sisters, can do to each other.

At Chaing Rai in northern Thailand, we visited the Opium Museum. The artwork, as we walked through a tunnel, and the sad music and darkness with little lighting, was powerfully moving. We toured for two distressing hours learning about the Opium Wars when Britain, and later the US and other countries, forced China to accept opium in exchange for Chinese tea.

In Cambodia we walked through the Killing Fields of the Pol Pot regime's horrendous violence to its own people in the early 70s. There I saw a human bone that had worked up through the earth. It lay amidst the freshness and hope of new green plants on which the sun shone brightly.

Someone who works in a Cambodian organization made the point that all these decades later, the entire country is still suffering from PTSD. That reality will stay with me, along with the courageous response that Pol Pot's sister gave when the US invited her and her other brother to come to live here after the war. She declined, saying that they needed to stay in Cambodia to pay for what Pol Pot had done in and to their country.

Peace: Humanity's New Art

In his book, *The Moral Imagination*, Jon Lederach says, **"The role of the artist is to move us to something new and unexpected while rising from and speaking to the everyday…This is the role of the artist…and why it is that imagination and art are at the edge of society – by being on the edge they push the edge of what is thought to be real and possible…"** He speaks about how vital it is to keep alive the **"ministry of imagination"** and to keep on conjuring and proposing future alternatives to what is.

When I studied as a Peace Fellow, the International Rotary President was Ravi Ravindran from Sri Lanka. He said, **"We cannot fight violence with violence. But when we fight it with education, with understanding and with peace, we can truly be a gift to the world."**

When making my initial classroom presentation shortly after arriving at Chulalongkorn University, I spoke about my work teaching conflict resolution skills to students in Midland and in area schools with Randi, Judy and Bruce. All are members of our local Nonviolent Peaceforce chapter that sponsors our **"Lessons in Leadership - Students Crafting Solutions"** program. It was great to know I would return home to this valuable, hopeful work that has included some new schools, plus new team members, Elaine, Kathleen and Sandy.

Hope is based in educating children and youth to understand that while conflict is a given element of human life, responding violently or nonviolently is a choice humans make as we deal with situations involving people from different cultures, generations, genders, perspectives and positions. Learning skills in one thing and crafting them into a healing way of life is an art that gifts the world with hope and beauty.

I refer to all current youth as Perennials, both those who are learning to practice nonviolent conflict resolution skills and others who hopefully will do so as the 21st Century unfolds. Their never-ending learning and practicing of such skills will help build a more peaceful world. They will then need to continue throughout their lives, to keep reminding others of its value and modeling this in the slow evolution toward creating a culture of peace.

We adults (many who did not grow up learning these skills) will **"be a gift to the world"** by teaching youth through modeling the importance of learning and practicing skills of preventing and of dealing with conflict nonviolently. Author Clarissa Pinkola Estés said, **"Children must pick up the burden of the unlived lives of their fathers or mothers."** A direct benefit of living a life that demonstrates that peace is humanity's new art, will be that children, youth and young adults can then be teachers for each other and to people of all age groups. Thus, the burdens of being human will be more fairly shared by all. This work will be perennial, as everyone does his or her best to help build and maintain a life-giving culture that a growing number of young people already understand is vital: **"We have inherited a large house, a great 'world house' in which we live together… a family unduly separated in ideas, culture and interests who, because we can never again live apart, must learn to live with each other in peace."** Martin Luther King Jr. 1964

In the **UN Declaration of the Rights of the Child**, two of the basic rights **"in the best interest of the children"** are education and the right to be brought up in the spirit of peace. The process of obtaining peace even within one country, let alone all the international challenges, is burdened with slowness, power struggles and backsliding, to name just a few. We adults have a lot of growing up to do to help assure that all children everywhere experience their basic human rights.

Wendy Helperin, Michigan author of *PEACE* and other children's books, says, **"In serving the best interest of the children we will serve the best interest of humanity.**

Life-Long Commitment

Two significant commitments that Peace Fellows in the professional development program are required to honor are:

1. to return home and continue work we have already been doing and
2. to be ambassadors for Rotary.

On arriving home I looked forward to returning to teaching conflict resolution and continuing mediation through the Community Resolution Center.

96

As for being an ambassador, I much prefer to think of myself as a cheerleader for Rotary. In high school when I wanted to be a cheerleader, Mom said I couldn't do that because those girls wore skirts that were too short. Now here I am a half-century later cheering on the healing and hopeful work of 33,000+ Rotary Clubs, the Rotary Action Group (RAG) for peace and hundreds of graduates of Rotary Peace Programs. Rotary is helping make peace happen worldwide. My gratitude for benefiting from this vision, legacy and generosity will be a life-long commitment. After speaking at a District 6310 Gala Dinner, I asked everyone to rise, then told them to give themselves a standing-ovation, a gesture that is fully deserved.

Collaborating with Rotary has already had hopeful outcomes. Recently our Midland Chapter of the Nonviolent Peaceforce has collaborated with Michigan District 6310 and local Clubs. NP member, Randi and I have met with the Noon Rotary Club's recently initiated Peace and Conflict Resolution Committee. Subsequently our Chapter brought in and hosted conflict resolution trainers for three sessions at which Rotarian Interactor, Rotaractor and adult club members participated along with NP Chapter members.

Elder Leadership - Changing Thinking

I agree with author Jon Lederach who believes that "**...if we are to survive as a global community, we must understand the imperative nature of giving birth and space to the moral imagination in human affairs. We must face the fact that much of our current system for responding to deadly local and international conflict is incapable of overcoming cycles of violent patterns precisely because our imagination has been** corralled and shackled by the very parameters and sources that create and perpetrate violence. **OUR CHALLENGE IS HOW TO INVOKE, SET FREE AND SUSTAIN INNOVATIVE RESPONSES TO THE ROOTS OF VIOLENCE WHILE RISING ABOVE IT."**

Albert Einstein's words echo this wisdom: **"The world as we have created it is a process of our thinking. It cannot be changed without changing our thinking."**

At my fellowship graduation I shared stories of this work that I am passionate about and included a Martin Luther King quote that continues to be a challenge to our thinking. **"This is the unusual thing about nonviolence. Nobody is defeated, everyone shares in the victory."**

I continued: **"To rise to this challenge necessitates taking a personal, very conscious journey on a path that circles and winds through each day of our lives. There is no retirement, and the energy to take the next step, no matter how tiny, no matter our age, is within us as we strive to align our daily habits of living to modeling the change we are called to be."**

There is a lot of work ahead for the growing population of elders. For humanity to evolve from win-lose to win-win outcomes requires transformation of our practices such as **"If he hits you, hit him back harder!"** Clearly looking at our world's history shows that this only leads to future problems that affect more people now and will in future generations. Elders have a lot to answer for and a lot to do because of damage done through centuries of thinking and actions that we have followed and justified.

I have been involved with peace issues since my kids Ann Marie, Peter, Matthew and Christopher were little. Since becoming a grandparent in 2001, shortly after 9/11, as a gift to Chloe, then to Easton and Dawson, I have focused more on peace and nonviolence as a way of life. In our program in schools, initiated in 2013, we help students understand that by drawing on their inner strength, they can change their thinking and thus their actions. Then they can help bring about change, and understand how the smallest positive gesture helps build peace, not just in their schools but beyond. We explain, for example, that when they see someone being bullied, they can choose between being a bystander or an upstander. As an elder, if I teach this without modeling it, I have failed them and increased the burden that they have to carry in the world.

I strongly believe that when kids grow up observing and experiencing win/win conflict resolution, they accept this as the norm, just as those who grow up in the midst of domestic violence often believe that is normal. If they grow up understanding that conflict is simply part of human relationships and that they have a part to play in creating positive resolutions, and if they consciously practice and support a win/win model of interchange, they will consider this as their own normal behavior and will expect it of others.

My experience as a Rotary Peace Fellow has deepened my belief that humanity is evolving in many hopeful ways and also that world citizens of all ages have lots of work to do to help build a better world for everyone. Maybe one of the reasons people are living longer is that we have a specific responsibility to lay life-giving groundwork for children everywhere and for those who are yet to be born. Partnering with our Creator God and with the Golden Rule believers of all religions or of no religion is a key element in the prescription needed personally, nationally and globally to move toward a win-win culture that benefits everyone. Since there's no magic wand way to accomplish this, it may be written off as totally naive, given the history of humankind. And yet there are hopeful signs all over the world on a daily basis, even in the midst of horrendous violence. There is much cause for hope and there are many unexpected life-giving surprises yet to come.

Life is a Mystery

Before graduating on August 27, 2015, Peace Fellows each posted a blog on the Rotary Peace program website. Mine ended: **"Life is a mystery. A year ago I had no idea if I would be chosen for this program…To my great delight I was chosen, to be in this place, at this time, with these people. The mystery deepens and the next page in my life is about to turn. That's all I need to know."**

On August 28th I headed home, pleased to be able to reconnect with family and friends and get on with my work. Part of being a cheerleader for Rotary is sharing what I called **"Gratitude and Glimpses"** of my experience, something that I was delighted to do. After returning home I gave approximately 15 presentations to Rotary Clubs and gatherings within District 6310 and to other groups and organizations.

One point that has been particularly important for me to make was tied in with the learning module that included conflict analysis. Peace Fellows wrote papers naming the Dividers and the Connectors within the work we do. That process helped me step back in order to recognize and name all the positive and negative elements in a situation. It also increased my admiration for Rotary and the vital international role it has embraced. With its six focuses: peace and conflict prevention/resolution, disease prevention and treatment, water and sanitation, maternal and child health, basic education and literacy, and economic and community development, all having international impacts, Rotary has definitely been a major connector and a tremendous gift to the world. I have been deeply blessed to have had such a life-changing experience.

Personal Evolution - Embracing Change

Nine months after returning from my Bangkok Adventure, I was once again aware that something was birthing in me regarding where should my focus be now? Should I continue to be an organizer heading up groups or should I step back and spend more time and energy connecting with people?

At the end of an organizing meeting for the 2016 International Day of Peace, I asked Linda for feedback. She immediately said: **"Making connections."** It was a blessing that her response came instantly because it resonated with what my heart was telling me. A couple years ago I had stepped down from heading the Choosing a Culture of Understanding group. Since that brief conversation with Linda it later became clear that I also needed to let go of heading the Helen M. Casey Center for Nonviolence. Our board members Marge, Norb and my husband George agreed that this was the choice to make. After almost 14 years, it officially closed with a celebration retreat in March 2017. Sister Brigid presented a talk about violence and climate change. Sister Goretti, a long-time friend of Helen's led the participants in Helen-memories. Both nuns are Grand Rapids Dominicans connected with my alma mater, Aquinas College. It was a rich blessing to have them present. It was a sad, and yet hopeful celebration as we closed the doors but not our hearts to the inspiration that Helen had been for decades to us and to many others.

In addition, as part of the Church of the Brethren's Ministry Team, I realized it was time to preach less. Although I was surprised that these two involvements would surface as let go possibilities, both decisions made perfect sense. I felt both sadness and relief. As more space births in me, I am waiting for further clarification and surprises to unfold.

Extravert or Introvert? What came to mind regarding needed changes was a Myers Briggs test from many years ago that showed that I am nurtured by equal amounts of both of those personality elements. Recalling this was a good reminder that I very much need a balance between connecting with people and organizations and creating plenty of quiet time and space. Is creating that better balance the current challenge I am to embrace as I move forward in this current growing-up phase?

Contrary to my earlier mode of **"I don't need to figure it out, but to let it unfold."** I have recently been aware of my **"I want the answer instantly!"** and other points of frustration and confusion. Thanks to spiritual direction and an Advent retreat at the prayer house, even though I dearly wish there were not so many questions floating around, burdening my mind/body/spirit, I am better able to accept that this major transition period will likely be a slow process.

Practicing personal rituals is a blessing in gaining perspective as I move onward.

Dancing Without a Script

A prayer that I have said for several years when beginning my morning stretching exercises has surely played a part towards stepping into the unknown. It was inspired by

Chakra teacher, Carolyn Myss. As I raise my arms high above my head while being mindful of my chakra energy flowing, I recite: **"Holy Spirit, I open myself to all the positive energy that is in the cosmos for me today. I invite it down through my sacred contract, down through my chakras to root me deeply in the earth and to help me dance in the cosmos without a script."**

In June of 2016 I journaled: **"Has praying this regularly been part of this current nudge to 'dance...without a script'? I love to dance. My body, mind and spirit thrive on it. However, since first reciting this prayer many years ago, I have known that it calls me to something far deeper. So this morning I asked myself if this positive energy flow that I'm praying for to help me dance without a script is both nudging and empowering me, after 70 years of living, to let go of my script, to let go of the ways I approach and do things that have for so long been scripted by my gifts as an organizer who very much enjoys figuring things out."**

Reviewing my personal history has helped. Organizing has been part of my DNA for a long time. In high school I was the first female Student Council President. I started writing as a teenager while working at the Oceana Herald in Shelby. These experiences were helpful in developing organizing skills and in figuring things out through interviewing and then writing about people in the community.

As a high school and college student in the 1960s, I had a clear sense of who I was and of some of the things I wanted to do. At age 71, I recall my dreams to be an interpreter for the UN that never happened. However, connecting with and studying with Peace Fellows from five continents and 12 countries during my Bangkok Adventure was in some way a realization of that dream. I never regretted not following that earlier one, and having this surprising gift come not in THE late 60s but in MY late 60s is an example of dancing in the cosmos without a script. I hadn't even imagined this would happen, so definitely didn't try to figure out how to make this life-changing experience unfold, but it did! Not only has it connected me personally with people from different countries, this experience has connected my heart more fully with people all over the world.

When I begin my outside morning walking/sitting meditation, I stop a minute in front of the Meta Buddha garden near our International Stone Wall and begin by naming George, Ann Marie, Guy, Peter, Michele, Chloe, Matt, Christopher, Jennifer, Easton and Dawson, then say, **"I bring with me all of our family, all of our neighbors, all of the Church of the Brethren, the Rotary Peace Fellows and their loved ones, anyone connected in any way with Rotary and with the Nonviolent Peaceforce."** When stepping onto the path that gently winds toward the prayer house, I'm mindful of being accompanied by a host of people worldwide.

On most days, my prayer and meditation come before other focuses, as early morning works best for me. The question coming to me in this regard is: Do I trust deep down that guidance for my decisions flows on a regular basis? Yes. I do. It's reassuring to realize that even when hoping for instant clarity, that deep inside there is an ever-growing trust in the mystery of life. An ongoing nudge by the Holy Spirit to **"Let go and Let God"** inspires me to embrace more fully my particular path as I strive, with all my faults, to do my best to live the way for which my Father/Mother God has created me.

A morning prayer to the Holy Spirit, shared by Mary, my dear friend and neighbor for almost 40 years helps to strengthen my daily commitment to live God's will:

O Holy and astounding Spirit,
You catch me by surprise at least once a day
With the freshness of your love
And the unpredictability of your presence – especially in humble
things that somehow give me immense joy.
Some moments are completely new, full of joy
As uplifting as the dawning sun,
And those moments come from you, day by day.
Stand behind me today when I'm right and
Ought to be more determined,
And block my way when I'm being
Stupid and ought to back off.
Teach me true compassion for those in need
So I can be of genuine help to someone.
Bless me today, Holy Spirit, and astound me again. Amen.

The Journey Continues

During a recent meeting with my spiritual director, Reverend Mary Jo, when I was sharing certain challenges, she reminded me that water rituals have long been significant in my life. She asked if I had done any lately. I was amazed that such a healing element had been forgotten. Going to Holland on the Lake Michigan side of the state to visit Kathy, the one who shared in my serenity ritual years ago on that rainy day at the prayer house, was already on my calendar. Knowing we would spend time on the beach, I created a ritual and Kathy joined me. It was a special blessing to share this special moment with such a special friend.

On that unseasonably warm, sunny November afternoon, after walking then sitting on the beach, we stood in the water of my favorite lake. The brief prayer was that whatever crud was in us might be washed out to make room for whatever newness was waiting to flow in. Naming my crud was easy. As to what would be flowing in, I had no desire or need to know. Waiting for that newness to unfold is part of the deep mystery of life as the journey continues.

Made in the USA
Lexington, KY
19 November 2017